Sunset House

Sunset House

Selected Essays

Marshall Moore

REBEL SATORI PRESS
New Orleans & New York

Book design: Sven Davisson

Paperback ISBN: 978-1-60864-324-0

Acknowledgments

The following originally appeared in:

Sunset House (*Storgy*, 5 September 2021)

The First Ghost I Ever Saw Was (*Your Impossible Voice*, Spring 2022)

A Knock on the Door in the Night (*Welter*, Vol. 57: Spring 2023)

The Screwdriver Pedagogies (*Autofocus*, April 6, 2022)

Storms and Boxes (*The Southern Review*, Vol. 58, No. 3, Summer 2022)

On Surveillance (*Angel Rust*, Issue 9, March 2022)

The Departure Board (*Passengers Journal*, Issue 3.1, March 2022)

The Fibonacci Grawlix (or: Bullshit Repellant) (*Identity Theory*, August 11, 2022)

Tardiness: A Personal History (*Queerlings*, Issue 4, 2021)

The Things We Take With Us Are Rarely the Things That We'll Need (*Trampset*, July 2023)

To the Barricades (or: Writers, Blocked) (*Untenured*, Issue 1, 2022)

The Afternoon Administration (*A Thin Slice of Anxiety*, May 13, 2022)

Tasting Notes (*Unfortunately Literary Magazine*, February 20, 2024)

Black Noon, Blue Evening (*Barren Magazine*, Issue 22, 2023)

Then, the White Noise (*Eunoia Review*, May 1, 2023)

CONTENTS

SUNSET HOUSE

Another evening, another livid sky. I'm gazing out my home-office window at the horizon again. Cornwall's towering clouds dwarf the shiny cotton balls that scud across the sky in my native eastern North Carolina. Backlit with electric danger, these massive clouds— slate blue grey and limned around the edges by the setting sun—are too big for simple shape names to fit. They're more like empires, or archipelagos. The sky fades through various shades of salmon and ultramarine. It's quite late, almost ten now. Night comes reluctantly here.

Off to the west and a bit to the south, atop the crest of a low hill, dots of red light strobe on a broadcasting tower. I see it every day and night but Google thinks it's not there. I've checked Maps and done a web search. Nothing shows up. I imagine the tower serves some arcane military purpose. Maybe it's a Cold War-era numbers station still spitting out synethesized digits for spies on passing ships. We're not far from the sea. This part of Cornwall is far from everything *but* the sea. Perhaps this idea isn't as far-fetched as it seems.

I moved here in 2020 after spending 12 years in Hong Kong. Unless you've been in hibernation, you will have seen the headlines and the carnage. Early on in the protests, a new thought formed in my head and stayed there: *I'm no longer sure I know who I am.* The notion of being lost to yourself recurs in song lyrics and literature.

1

I always scorned it as a pop-music cliche: rhyming angst in a trite, saddish chorus. At some point I stopped getting so wound up about things like that; as an adult, I have more age-appropriate concerns. Even so, when friends and relatives found themselves in relationships they'd sacrificed cherished parts of themselves to maintain, a bit of that contempt would glimmer in the back of my mind. *How could you let that happen? What were you thinking? What's wrong with you?* Since karma doesn't miss much, naturally I ended up as one of those people myself.

When the final digit of your age is 9, you'll have questions. Possibly fears as well, depending on your circumstances. For me, those transitions have always been upgrades. I enjoyed being 19 because my teenage years were awful and would end soon. Turning 29 came as a relief because my 20s were a decade-long struggle to overcome disasters past and present. Good goddamn riddance. I liked 39 because although my 30s were better on average, there was the shattering breakup, the financial implosion, and the ensuing nervous breakdown. I only stayed out of the hospital because I'd just written a novel about that and didn't want to be a case of life imitating art. My 40s were actually sort of okay. Then I found myself at 49 in a burning Golgotha of tear gas, mass arrests, and urban warfare. As events there spiralled beyond what I thought it would be possible to live through, that question intensified: *Who the hell have I turned into?*

Some of it was simple stuff, the kind of thing you take stock of after a decade with the person you'll go on to marry. My partner-now-husband didn't like my wardrobe full of grey and black clothes and pushed me to explore the virtues of color. He worked in fashion, upper management. I attempted to teach essay skills and grammar to yawning college students. I told myself it was okay to let my boyfriend be right about things now and then. Years passed. While I didn't hate the plaids and checks and other patterns, they didn't look like *me*, and when Hong Kong's protest movement adopted black (bloc) as its emblem of resistance and mourning, something clicked.

What other compromises had I made for the relationship? What else had I changed? Certain things were much-needed improvements. A year after S. and I got together, I had half a dozen ugly moles lasered off my back. I didn't like them, but I didn't have to see them every day. They grossed him out, though. One session at a skin clinic later, they were gone. I didn't miss them. I still don't. But: *Did I actually alter my body for this man? Isn't that the kind of thing I swore never to do?* I also stopped getting tattoos, or put it on pause. How much of that was about never getting around to it; how much was about his vague revulsion? Yet that coil of uncertainty stayed in its subcellar, twisting amid a growing lack of recognition: *Who have I become? Who am I becoming?* And as the images on TV got worse with every passing week, as everyone we knew got gassed and finally we did too, as I ran from cops to avoid getting beaten and arrested, as we had the inevitable "what has to happen to make us grab the cat and go to the airport?" discussion, as I sat crying and often drunk in my armchair in the living room watching fires and brawls and tear gas canisters shot at civilians in metro stations on TV, as the cops collectively lost their minds and went on the rampage, as the rumors of murder and rendition and gang rape and dismemberment spread, I kept coming back to that question. That simple, unanswerable question: *Who am I?* The answer: *I am surviving this.* No longer a person but a process.

Then the pandemic started.

I took a year off in college to, as my mother tended to moan in a Valium-laced haze to anyone still listening, find myself. I started university at age 16 and would have graduated at 20 had I not taken that year off and flunked a few classes along the way. I'd just come out. It was traumatic. If you were one of those kids who get bullied relentlessly at school and home's not much better, you'll know what I mean. So much work goes into constructing an identity based on the negation of something both painful and painfully obvious. Worse, straight people think you're flaming if you're even slightly legible as gay. The decision feels made already, *fait accompli*, imposed long before you're ready. That year I took off was less about searching than it was about shoveling away the silt of inauthenticity I was suffocating under. Self-abnegation is exhausting. But I couldn't explain any of this to my mother. Newly divorced and full of cascading emptiness, she drank, took pills, and fell down a lot. She'd surrendered an identity at the altar, and now that her marriage was over, all she found inside was a darkness and the urge to scream.

Being American means you tend to conflate who you are with what you do. I learned that at an early age even if it took moving overseas to begin untangling some of those threads. Like any bookish, gifted gay university student used to being good at everything that didn't involve human interaction, I smugly thought all questions had been answered. I was out, I was relieved, and I was free to go on being the sum of my accomplishments past present and future rather than this hiding, cringing other thing. I'd always had a strong sense of self. But during this interval, another question emerged: Can you really know yourself when your life has been so focused on that pivotal task of not-being?

During this time, I took a lot of long late-afternoon drives through the countryside. The best time for these drives was around six, after the heat of the day and the silver-grey glare off the clouds had retreated, but before it got dark—and before my mother's drunken, screaming meltdowns or fits of near-catatonic depression would commence for the evening. I knew those roads well; I'd lived in that part of the state most of my life. I knew how fast I could go, how well the tires would adhere to the pavement on certain curves, where speed traps were likely to be. There were fewer shit lagoons— the massive tanks of manure created by industrial hog farming— back then, so the air was fresh except around the big Weyerhaeuser pulp mill off highway 43 on the way to New Bern. Now and then I'd take the ferry across the Pamlico River from Aurora to Bayview, and circle back home from there. There were seagulls to feed. Cute backwoods gas stations where I could stop for a Pepsi and a candy bar. Even if I was speeding, I wasn't in a hurry. The journey itself was the destination, even if I sometimes got a little bit lost.

The seagulls stop their bickering at sunset. The racket they make still feels like an anomaly. Being from a coastal region, I've heard that sound all my life. On ferries, my mother loved to tell and retell the story of how her father liked getting seagulls drunk. He would plan in advance, soaking bread in beer before tossing it off the back of the boat. The birds would get hammered, flop around the air, and fall into the water. "*KerPLOP!*," she would screech. Heads would turn. Lacking self-awareness, she would burst into benzodiazepine giggles at her own punchline, repeating it to get us to laugh too, which, as we got older, tended to happen less.

I did my PhD at Aberystwyth, a charming seaside college town in Wales even more remote than where I live now. Fittingly, the main road there is Great Darkgate: it ends at the ruins of a castle, well lit at night. A wide promenade arcs along the seafront. At low tide, the seabed is a lunar scramble of jagged rock. From time to time, storms blow in off the Irish Sea and batter the town with waves the size of houses. Rocks as well: the waves hurl them ashore, smashing windows out of buildings and cars. It's spectacular, at least if you can watch from the comfort of YouTube. The gulls of Aberystwyth are the size of tablecloths, almost as white, and rapacious. They will take your food. They will shit on your head. Fear them.

During my time there—I was a part-time student and stayed in Hong Kong for the degree, travelling to Wales once or twice a year per the uni's requirement—I was always in a fog of exhaustion and cognitive dissonance. *How am I actually here right now, doing this? Someone's going to find out. Good things are not allowed to happen.* In the library, I'd often nod off in an armchair, doze for a few minutes, then jerk awake, pat my chin to check for drool, and look around to see if anyone was watching. I'd look out the narrow window I always sat next to. There was a view of the sea. *What am I even doing here?* Isolation, containment, seagulls. It was a strange time but rather lovely in its contours.

With Covid restrictions still in force—the recent G7 conference has left Cornwall sloshing with the virus—just writing about the pandemic feels repugnant, as if I'm forcing myself to swallow food I know is spoiled. But with winter finally over, I've had a lot of time to reflect on isolation. I arrived in England toward the end of a lockdown, taught one semester on campus but have no idea what the students look like because they were all wearing masks, and spent the spring semester online, barely leaving my house. Full dark by half four, often pouring. Not much chance for exercise. When I lived in Seattle and Portland, I thought the clouds and rain were amazing. Everything about that time in my life was collapses and setbacks, but I could take unmasked breaths at Whole Foods without fear of dying in a plague ward three weeks later. I have never cared as much about sunlight as I do now, especially as the last of it bleeds into night.

Toward the end of Hong Kong's summer of protests, I got an email from someone whose name I didn't recognize right away. I was on my way home, about halfway up the Mid-Levels Escalator. I called that part of Hong Kong Airless Hill because even by the standards of the city's miserable swelter, a trip up that system of travellators felt like the journey a lump of dough makes through an industrial oven. Chilly in tone, the email was a notification that my mother had developed dementia and was no longer capable of taking care of herself. Arrangements had already been made.

The air was acrid with tear gas the next day when I replied to find out more. The gist was that this woman, a longtime friend of my mother's, was now her power of attorney—a role I thought had been assigned to me. There was a second POA: a former gentleman friend of hers. I'd heard of him. He was married the entire time the affair lasted. Still was, as far as I knew. Things happened fast after that: they listed the house with an estate agency and put the car up for sale, contacted someone in Raleigh to come down and auction the antiques, and set about emptying her bank accounts. An alarmed distant cousin tracked me down when he heard the news. Was this legit? Live in eastern North Carolina long enough, you'll hear stories of estate grabs like this. I hired a lawyer. Did some checking. The US's brutal sham of a health care system demands that everything be liquidated before Social Security will kick in and cover the cost of a care home. In North Carolina, there's a seven-year window prior to the time of admission to the facility. The system only kicks in after your assets are spent down. They'll demand your financials and claw back anything you've stashed in a trust. And the will my mother had given me a copy of? Not valid, apparently. It wasn't notarized, something she would have known about after her decades as a notary public.

With every email and every phone call, the situation grew more sordid. My mother's former companion disapproved of my gallivanting gay lifestyle, was appalled that I was living overseas and not back in my hometown doting on the malignant narcissist who was very good at performing normal (but we don't talk about that because in our South you don't), and was adamant that I be kept out of the process. The other friend, the one who contacted me, agreed and went along with it. She too thought I was deplorable. I could tell from the frost in her voice when we spoke. But at some point her conscience caught up with her. I deserved to be told, even if she couldn't stand me.

Week after week, things got worse. The news from North Carolina, the news from Hong Kong. Fresh bombardments: The former gentleman friend took indecent liberties with my mother; Adult Protective Services had to be brought in. There was a restraining order. He was barred from the facility where she was now living. He barged in anyway. I think the cops were called. Molotov cocktails: The lawyer assured me there was absolutely nothing I could do. It would take everything I had to chase after things I had already lost. Long since lost, and in all honesty, never had. The relationship, the items in the will. Things I thought were true. The former gentleman friend stole some of her jewelry and tried to take her car. He got in trouble for it but he had paperwork and I was in Asia. Strong hurricanes hit both places.

My sister, who moved out at age 18 and proclaimed herself done, put it succinctly: "She fucked you out of six figures. She's done something like this to literally every person in her life. You're the last. Walk away."

No one does the unthinkable without first having endured it. There was a time in my life I would have rushed back to North Carolina to do something. The problem was, this time there was nothing I could actually do. It had already happened. Everything: gone in the space of a few days, the mother, the lifetime of lies, the estate. Lacking other options, I'd have even consented to it all if I'd been given any say in the matter. That was taken away from me too. I spoke to her on the phone once. She wasn't sure who I was. Reluctantly and with real grief, I took my sister's advice.

Not long after that, the Teachers' March, one of the dozens of individual protests that hideous summer and fall, took place in Hong Kong. It started on a muggy, stifling morning and took us up a steep hill to the Chief Executive's residence near the American consulate. The marchers were turned away at the top, leaving the whole contingent to file down a single hillside staircase instead of continuing as planned. As a kid and in young adulthood, I swore I'd

9

never become a teacher. Too risky if you're gay. Time moved on, of course, and so did I, finding myself in a crowd of 22,000 black-clad, balaclava'd colleagues as we filed slowly down that hill that blistering day, two by two.

Hungry and fried, my husband and the friend who'd joined us stopped for dim sum in Admiralty. The friend, a British Hong Konger, was blasé about the skin lesions she'd developed from over-exposure to tear gas. The depleted American canisters had been used up. Now the cops were using toxic new shit from China. Doctors all over the city were enraged because the government would not disclose the ingredients. They were tired of not knowing how to treat the casualties that poured into emergency rooms every week. The *har gao* and *siu mai* were exquisite. Half the patrons in the restaurant were also wearing black.

Even before all that, I wasn't always sure I could recognize myself in the mirror. Now, that man is gone. I'm someone else. Or perhaps I don't have to find myself because I've never not known who I am: a cold amalgam of loss, boarding passes, and survival. These persistent questions are the glue that hold the absences together, the white spaces on the pages of the story. I may never set foot in my hometown again. Nor do I expect to set foot in my adopted home. Neither thing would be safe. Here's one of the secrets of trauma: it's fucking boring. The terror and horror give way to a dull, ashy nothingness. You can survive anything when it's just nothingness that you have to survive.

I'm looking out the window of my home office again. It's almost eleven: fully dark now, no clouds in sight. Everything has been stripped away. From me, from the day. Whoever I am, I think I'm done now. It's finally night.

THE FIRST GHOST I
EVER SAW WAS

1.

The first ghost I ever saw was a column of golden light at the foot of my bed. I was nine or ten. There was no doubt in my mind it was real. Ghosts *were* real. Both parents said so. My grandmother too. When her newborn son, the baby boy who would have been my uncle, died in his crib, a trio of ghosts appeared at the foot of her own bed. She recognized them all. They were family, women who had already passed but were back now to escort this sick child to farther shores. One look at them and she knew he wouldn't make it through the night. My parents had seen ghosts too, had sent and received psychic messages, had kept careful biorhythm records for years. There was a Ouija board in one of the downstairs closets. My sister and I were under strict orders never to touch it, so of course we did. Somewhere in the house, we had a deck of Zener cards. This was our reality.

This first ghost would shimmer into being late at night, after I had gone to bed but before I fell asleep. It would linger, curiously flat, just at the edge of my vision. If I opened my eyes and sat up in bed, it would vanish. But if I waited long enough, squinting into the dark through half-shut eyes, in time it would reappear: silent, flickering, gleaming but somehow roiling, shot through with a paisley lacework of darkness. I wasn't afraid of it, not exactly. Even at that age, I was as rational as anyone in that context was going to be. If the ghost meant to hurt me, it had passed up plenty of chances.

By day, to stave off boredom in school, I considered possibilities. Ghosts tended to appear in old houses and other buildings, or along lonely highways. Perhaps you could see one drifting along a stretch of treacherous railroad track, or clinging vaporously to a widow's walk atop one of the old houses on the riverfront down in New Bern. But we lived in a new-build house in a neighborhood with a golf course and a country club. Although the fairways out beyond the treeline at the back of our yard could be misty and creepy late at night, as could the swamps they adjoined, the house hadn't been around long enough for anyone to have died there. I was certain of this.

What about distant dead relatives? There seemed to be no lack of them. The baby uncle, dead in his crib. Spinal meningitis took the little girl who would have been my aunt if she'd survived. My father's sister. And on my mother's side, there was the great aunt who'd been struck down by a car one Christmas night. Her own car broke down. She was walking to get help. Someone hit her and kept going. Ever after, sadness festooned the holidays. Since more of our family seemed to be dead than alive, it seemed possible one of them wanted to reach me. I just didn't know what they might want to say.

2.

A darkness had always surrounded our house. Locked boxes, empty rooms. Secrets hinted at but never discussed. My sister (we'll call her J.) and I were characters in our own ghost story as it played out in the modern manor house in the country-club suburbs. There was no fence between our back yard and the golf course. I never knew where the property line was. The yard was a ragged patch of grass, never landscaped, that merged into a dense scribble of woodland and briars. One side was almost impassable, but you could walk toward the pond and back through the trees to get to the fairways. There were two ponds: ours and the one on the golf course. The stumps of four dead trees jutted up from the one that formed a water trap between the 8th hole and the 9th. Lightning struck one of them not long after we moved in, left it charred and smoking. An electric charcoal reek hung over the neighborhood all the next day. Blackened splinters and twigs floated in the brown water until the country club sent a man with a boat to skim off the flotsam. We could go out and explore the golf course on our bikes. There was very little contact with other kids, though. Our parents didn't socialize and didn't want to. A heavy sadness hung in the air, and the silences were the kind that echoed after shouts and the sound of slapped faces.

Like most troubled kids, I thought constantly about running away from home. Although I didn't *think* I'd go through with it, we sometimes couldn't go to swim practice until the bruises faded. Both parents were often drunk, and had guns. Although I didn't *think* they were going to kill us, Mom had already told me of their plan to do just that. If the Russians dropped the bomb, she once told me, everything would be terrible afterward, unlivable. So our parents had decided that the night civilization ended, they were going to shoot J. and me in our sleep, and then themselves. We could then be together as a family. Permanently.

When I got old enough, I'd sneak out at night and go for long walks. Practice runs, so to speak. Could I creep out without making the floors squeak, or the stairs? Well, yes, it was a new house. We had sliding glass doors. Outside, it didn't matter how much noise I made. I'd tromp through the woods to the golf course. In fall, ground fog would seep up from the earth and eddy around my feet. During our first year in that house, I had gone through a phase—just a week or two—of having an imaginary friend. Being older and a bit horrified by my own lonely awkwardness then, I cringed when I looked back on this. Perhaps if I'd ever been able to settle on a name for this imaginary boy who liked me for some unknowable reason and chose to stick around, I'd have been less appalled. But I could never decide what to call him. Before long, he retreated to the back corners of my mind, anonymous if not forgotten altogether. Now, with leaves rustling underfoot and twigs snapping, thin mist swirling around my ankles, I didn't feel so embarrassed. Having someone who didn't exist to walk through the woods with me would have been very welcome.

Being as rational in that context as anyone was going to be, I kept to the middle of the greens. One side of the course didn't scare me at all: the side where the houses were. Hedges and low split-rail fences separated the links from the back yards. Clumps of azaleas and stands of ornamental pampas grass formed some of those borders. My family's patch of woods didn't scare me much either. However, the far side of the course butted up against a forest wall of swamp.

The manicured grass formed a sharp boundary on the other side of which were tangles of briars and deep mud. If you could push your way through the thickets without shredding your flesh, you'd find yourself on ground that sloped down into the dark. Cypress knees poked up from pools of black, stagnant water. There were snakes and mosquitoes. Clumps of poison oak. Gigantic frogs the size of your foot. Possibly alligators.

And the ghosts. Nothing visible, of course, just the weight of unseen eyes following your progress across the grass and into the swamp if you were brave or insane enough to try that at night, which I wasn't. I sometimes walked along the paved golf-cart lane to see where I'd end up. Once, I saw a human figure off in the distance, or imagined I did. The fingernail moon cast very little light. If there was someone there watching me, he merged back into the trees when I tried to look closer. He might have been dead and come back to menace me; he might have been alive and intending the same. Preferring the safety of familiar dangers, I hurried home.

3.

The best ghost stories involve glimpses at twilight, whispers in darkening rooms, hints of madness. Doubt spirals; gaslights flicker. A sense of unease rolls in like the fog. According to my grandmother, the Croatan National Forest near New Bern was one of the most haunted places in the country. Since the earliest days of colonial history, the eastern end of the state has had issues with people going missing. An entire colony of British settlers vanished back in the late

1500s, leaving behind the word CROATOAN carved into a perimeter fence, and little else. Much of eastern North Carolina is swampland. Barrier islands—the Outer Banks—absorb the worst of the hurricane damage, but the coastal mainland has drowned time and again. It's a desolate area, sparsely populated. Shadows, tree branches garlanded with Spanish moss, tumbledown gravestones behind abandoned churches like broken teeth in rotten gums. Legend has it there are plenty of ghosts.

If the Great Dismal Swamp forms eastern North Carolina's northern boundary, the Cape Fear River is arguably its southern one. These names cast an apt, descriptive pall over that end of the state, and every town seemed to have its own stories: Bath, Beaufort, New Bern, Nags Head, Ocracoke, Arapahoe. The ghost of the vicious pirate Edward Teach—more commonly known as Blackbeard—was said to appear near his former home, perhaps searching for his severed head. The cemetery in New Bern where many of our family were buried was said to be haunted. The main gate wept, drops of water that felt like human tears. If one hit you when you passed through with a group, you'd be the next to die. Even the church next door to some family friends' house was said to be haunted: if you waited in the cellar long enough, objects would be thrown at you; if you squinted into the gloom, you might see a human-like shape coalesce, drifting toward you.

Over the years, the details of the stories ebbed and flowed with each telling. My grandfather died and came back shortly thereafter, manifesting in a cloudy state at the top of the staircase in the house where he'd lived. The Little Red House on Johnson Street, my mother called it. She and my grandmother would smell pipe smoke, the same tobacco he liked, and see a dim figure forming in the sunlight on the landing of the stairs. Missing him, they'd hurry up to stand in it before he disappeared again. There were the mysterious lights in the Great Dismal Swamp, not too far away, maybe an hour. Now and then we'd drive through it on the way to Norfolk or Williamsburg. Highway 17 skirts the eastern border of the protected area. Coming back at night, we'd squint out the car windows into the darkness, straining to see spectral flashes. The name of the place imparted a sense of menace. Every time we passed by, we'd remember the warnings: Never go in there. The waters are deep. There are no roads, no settlements. There are wild animals, things that will eat you. You'll get lost and you'll die. It stood to reason scores of other people *had* died, so we made sure to lock the car doors on each of these trips. We never stopped.

My adult self finds the details apocryphal if not the stories themselves. Except in upheavals, bedrock doesn't shift. How could that apparition have been my grandfather when my mother didn't live in that house at the time? He died when I was an infant. We lived in a different city then. Was it her own grandfather? That would have made more sense. And those pulsing lights I thought I saw once or twice in the depths of the Great Dismal Swamp as we sped by. Those could have been… but no, I'm not convinced I imagined it all. Our reality was cracked and tattered at the edges, and it stayed that way, the real bedrock.

4.

There's a story I like to tell about the moment I knew I was a writer:

elementary school, a creative writing assignment I read aloud, applause from my classmates when I was done, the realization I knew I was good at this and meant to do it. But that's not the whole story.

Not long after that success, I wrote another story. Halloween was right around the corner. October Down East is crisply glorious, almost a caricature of what autumn in America should be. The summer's miserable humidity drops away, the skies clear, and nights are cool enough for fires. Winter will be a cold, rainy grey mess but that's still a couple of months away. In the meantime, there will be bales of hay, the last of the tobacco curing sweetly in barns, endless leaves to rake. Back in the '70s and early '80s, stores didn't put up Christmas decorations on the 5th of July like they do now. You could enjoy the autumn for its own merits, not as foreplay before Father Christmas comes. With all those paper ghosts and skeletons and vampires as inspiration, and pumpkins gently rotting on every other porch, I felt inspired.

My first ghost story involved a lot of setup. At the time, my mother was a real-estate agent. I saw the inside of a lot of empty houses. When she took us along for showings, we'd explore them top to bottom. I don't recall anything menacing us. There would be dust swirling in afternoon slants of sunlight, and the occasional vacant cobweb. Crows outside because there were always crows. Vaguely disappointed nothing creepy ever materialized, I channeled this into a story. I've forgotten the beginning of the story since then. It's no loss. But the climax and anticlimax have stayed with me. The characters discover (o horror!) a skull hanging from the eaves outside, empty eye sockets gazing in at them. Exclamation points and screaming ensue. The end.

"That's *all?*" asked one of my classmates after I finished reading it aloud.

Everyone looked bored.

"Well, yeah? A skull? Isn't that scary?"

"No."

I learned a lesson about being a writer that day, but it wasn't the storytelling experience that cemented things for me. Yes, the disappointment stung. Where was the applause? It wasn't that I felt entitled to it. But the baseline was usually some baseline of "you talk funny" or "you walk funny" or "are you a queer?", and I wanted to be not terrible at something, to have a respite from the frantic sadness that was already gnawing at me, even at that age.

A few weeks or months after that, my friend Johnny came over for a sleep-over. When he took his overnight bag upstairs, my father pulled me aside for a warning: "No ghost stories. Ghosts scare him. His parents told me on the phone."

I didn't believe him. In fact, it might have been the first time in my life I flat-out refused to accept he was telling the truth. How could he be? After a lifelong immersion in what my sister now calls "the family woo-woo," I thought ghosts were normal and expected. Besides, we barely visited other people's homes. I assumed everybody had Ouija boards and books from Nostradamus and Edgar Cayce in the house. Wasn't that just... how things worked? Especially in the South, where someone had bled out on every square inch of real estate at some point in the past?

"I'm going to tell you a story," I told Johnny that night. "It's about the Wind Ghost." I'd like to say I scared a puddle of piss out of him, but I didn't. It wasn't much of a story, barely an improvement over that skull improbably suspended from the gutter of some idiot's house. I didn't get very far into it because the phrase "the Wind

Ghost" popped into my head but nothing else did. I tried to improvise but gave up: I knew the story wasn't a story, just a half-baked idea. More like a quarter. He didn't cry. I thought that was the end of it.

Somehow my father found out afterward, and beat the shit out of me. It wasn't the worst belting I ever got, but it was solidly in the top five. That's how I knew I was going to be a writer, or already was one.

5.

Being a teenager is difficult even when your mother is not a self-professed powerful telepath, medium, and clairvoyant. We were under constant psychic—or psychotic, as it were—surveillance. She claimed to know everything we were thinking, everything we did, everything we wanted to do. However, outside of the home, we couldn't talk about that, just as we couldn't ask our father questions about Vietnam. He'd survived the war in the sense that his body returned to America intact and more or less functioning. But between the ears, there was a screaming black static that he numbed with regular hangovers. He couldn't talk about his experiences there. He could barely talk. He could drink, though. The list of off-limits subjects didn't stop there, either. We couldn't talk about Vietnam; we also couldn't talk about his family down in Louisiana, none of whom we'd met. There was some unspeakable, undiscussable tragedy surrounding his mother's death. Something involving a car crash. She and her husband, my grandfather, ran off the road. The car caught on fire. He was thrown free, but she couldn't escape from the flames.

"But didn't she have a manicure set in her purse?" I would ask from time to time. My mother had one. There were nail clippers, cuticle scissors, that kind of thing. She kept the kit in her purse with the gun and the bottle of Valium. "Couldn't she have cut through the seatbelt strap and gotten free?"

"I think she was knocked out."

"But she must have had *something*, right?"

"Be that as it may." The Southern phrase to smother further discussion. It was never the logistics of her mother-in-law's death she wanted to talk about it, it was what followed: "I was dead asleep, and something woke me up. It was like being wrapped in a cold grey blanket. I knew something had happened to her. I just *knew*. And when the phone rang right after that, I already knew who was calling. When your father answered the phone and heard the news, he just turned white as a sheet. Bless his heart."

Being as rational as anyone in that context was going to be, I figured that if she could do all that, I probably could as well. I was already reading Stephen King, Clive Barker, and other horror writers, less for excitement than guidance. Maps of the familiar, as it were. I was writing stories, too. Terrible ones, no doubt: there was the tsunami of bacteria that washed away some prissy germophobes, and there was a garden-variety poisoning story involving a large amount of rosemary from the characters' back yard. Since I hadn't had much luck with the Zener cards, I latched onto the one other thing I could test: the Ouija board. She said she could get it to work by herself, no seance table of nervous friends needed. I decided to give it a try.

Over the next several years, I went through phases of using the board. By myself, I couldn't get the planchette to move unless I shoved it around on the board on purpose to spell out profanities. If I had J. or a couple of friends, though, we got different results. We kept our fingers light. I was strict about that. Not every session was a horror-movie success, of course, but enough questions got answers that we couldn't unsee the weird pattern.

In my freshman year of college, I used the Ouija board for the last time. I was in somebody's dorm room with friends. Beers had been had. And I made the grievous mistake of trying to summon my grandmother. One or two of the guys knew the whole story, but not all of them. When the planchette began to inch its way from letter to letter, there was the inevitable "whoa, dude, what the fuck?" moment. Then it got worse. We weren't talking to my grandmother, but to her murderer.

She didn't die in a car wreck.

"You should probably not use that thing again," my father advised in a rare moment of coherence. "I don't know who or what you were talking to, but it knew things. I do think Ouija boards work. We just don't know who's on the other end of the line. I think they can retrieve information from our heads. For your own safety, you should leave it alone."

That time, I took his advice.

6.

In the years that followed, I found more distance from the cauldron of material I'd grown up in. One way or another, as foretext or subtext, the ghoulies and ghaesties and long-leggedy beasties went into my fiction, most of which has since been published. A series of unpleasant events—the mundane kind, no ectoplasm or moaning apparitions in the night—saw me ricochet from North Carolina up to DC, then to the West Coast, from Oakland up to Portland and then Seattle, and then on to Korea before settling in Hong Kong, where I spent more than a decade.

In Hong Kong, ghosts were suddenly front and center in my life again. How much of that was Chinese culture and how much was just my superstitious partner-now-husband? All these years later, I've decided there's no clear demarcation. Before I moved into my first apartment there, in a 42-story highrise overlooking Victoria Harbour, S. insisted we perform a cleansing ritual. He instructed me to buy oranges, red candles, a sheaf of hell money, bags of candy, and some pork. The oranges would serve as candle holders. I had to put one in each corner of the flat. In the center, we'd burn the hell money as an offering. It serves as currency in the afterlife: the higher the denomination, the happier the ghosts will be. The candy was meant to be scattered around the center of the room. I'm murky now on what the pork was for. I think we left it in its package until the ceremony was over, then threw it away, the garbage can being a debased and secondary ritual portal to the beyond.

I also had to buy a broom for the ashes, a dustpan, and of course a fireproof bucket.

It was as messy as it sounds.

Did I do it because the ghosts were real? If I'm honest, no. It's not that I didn't believe in them, but Hong Kong's ghosts don't require authentication from American expats. Ghosts in Chinese culture have more agency than Western ones do. They can manifest as material beings. They can affect the physical world. They can eat and have sex and, if not placated, cause a great deal of harm. Western ghosts are less substantial, perceptible via only one or two senses: visible, perhaps, and accompanied by a chill; or only as a disembodied voice; or as a fragrant cloud of pipe smoke in a sunbeam. They return to places of significance and repeat actions almost as if programmed to do so. This is both boring and tragic, not scary. On the whole, Chinese ghosts get the better deal. They can enjoy a meal, get drunk, fuck, and then fuck shit up if they want to. Hence the need for regular, routine appeasement measures. It's not that any of this mattered to me, but it mattered very much to my boyfriend, so I did it.

I did the cleansing ritual at the next apartment too, over in Tsim Sha Tsui, just on the other side of the harbor from where I spent my first four years there. As nearly as I can tell, the first ritual made no difference whatsoever in my quality of life there. I had a major health scare, endured a terrible job followed by an even worse one, got illegally sacked, and had to take that employer to court. Quite a change from the misty fairways and bizarre apparitions and bruises on the back of my legs from childhood. Perhaps without these interventions, my circumstances would have been worse? In any case, the new apartment was on Prat Avenue, a street lined with sidewalk restaurants and bars. On weekends, it was crowded by five and loud until three. As if that weren't enough, at the end of the block, right across from my building, a karaoke bar installed speakers outdoors to entice or deafen passersby. That November, they put Mariah Carey's "All I Want for Christmas Is You" on an endless loop at full volume. It was a direct portal to one of the lower circles in Dante's hell. It was also what convinced me to put my foot down when the landlady sold the flat for some twenty times what she'd paid for it and

I had to move again. At the new flat—back on Hong Kong Island this time, over in semi-suburban Quarry Bay—I decided to take my chances and skip the ceremony. The smoke made my eyes and my throat sting, the ashes and melted candle wax made a godawful mess on the floors, and despite all that ritual supplication, I had still ended up driven to the edge of a screaming breakdown by a Christmas hit.

Hong Kong's ghosts occupy prime real estate in the culture there. You can walk down almost any street in the urban parts of the city and smell the smoke from burning paper on certain holidays. Shopkeepers haul their braziers out onto the sidewalk, stuff colorful sheafs of hell money in, give it a few squirts of lighter fluid, and toss a match in. The next day, you'll see blobs of solidified red wax next to the charred spots where the fires were. The mystical is part of the very infrastructure of the place: there are little shrines built into many buildings right at sidewalk level. Reflective tiles, pots of ash and burnt-down incense sticks, the stumps of a few candles. These are everywhere. Ghosts manifest in the business world too: a couple of the major property agencies have pages on their websites that list apartments people have died in. The information given includes the age and sex of the decedent, the manner of death, and for suicides, the motivation. These flats are thought to be haunted. Because of the obscene cost of living there, these tend to be bargains, relatively speaking. Before I moved there, I wouldn't have thought of ghosts (even the malevolent kind) as being helpful, but as it turned out, we had more reason to be scared of the living than the dead.

The first ghost I ever saw was in my B&B in Aberystwyth, Wales. I did my PhD at Aberystwyth but commuted from Hong Kong, as one does. Each time I went, I'd stay the requisite week at the same waterfront guest house, one of a colorful terrace along S. Marine Terrace. I never got a room with a sea view, a mercy considering what the storms there are like. Despite all the horror stories that surround the process of getting a PhD, for me it was more like writing another book with yearly trips to remote coastal Wales thrown in to keep things interesting. (The horror descended every time I got a bill for my tuition fees.)

For my research, I focused on ghost stories. Before starting the program, I didn't realize that ghost-story purists—scholars as well as genre enthusiasts—saw the form as distinct from horror. Ghost stories, as I've mentioned already, were meant to be about the fleeting glimpse, the mounting sense of dread. Hints, withholding, delicate reveals, implications of madness. In contrast, horror was vulgar: monsters shambling, blood splattering the walls, psychopaths slashing virgins with kitchen utensils. Flashiness, not the dignified restraint of Henry James and Algernon Blackwood.

On my final trip to Aberystwyth, the proprietress put me in the same room I'd stayed in the first time. I was there for my viva (or defense, as Americans would call it). The research was done, the writing was done, and this would be it. I was meeting friends for dinner and wanted to take a shower before going back out. It was early evening. The sun was still up. In the shower, I got a strong, prickly sense of someone watching me: the same subtle weight of a gaze I felt so many times back in North Carolina late at night. This seemed unlikely, as there were two doors to my room: an outer fire door that let into a landing on the stairs plus an inner one that served no clear purpose. I kept them locked. No one could have come in. But the feeling persisted. I finished, rinsed off, and dried myself quickly. As soon as I stepped out of the shower stall, that feeling intensified. Somebody else was in my room.

"Hello?"

Then I saw it: not a human form, exactly, but a sort of curvature to the air. I could see it out of the corner of my eye, in the same way you can see things at night as long as you don't look straight at them. When I looked slantwise, I could see it moving through the room toward a window. Then it was gone.

An hour later, I still had goosebumps.

Later, I asked the proprietress if the house was haunted.

"Oh, of course! We started seeing it as soon as we moved in. Now and then it moves the books around on the shelves. I had to have a word with it about knocking teacups over. It doesn't bother the dogs. You'd think it would."

"It hasn't tried to harm anyone, has it?"

She made a dismissive raspberry sound and waved a hand. I decided to let it go at that. On previous visits, I'd gotten a peculiar vibe in that room, but it wasn't my first encounter with ghosts that had passed up opportunities. I've long been familiar with the comfort of safer dangers. And as long as I had a few pints with dinner, I thought sleeping ought not to be too much trouble. Jet lag is a good mixer.

Before that, I'd never thought much about ghosts having helped me, but they have. Even the malevolent ones. I've turned out about as rational as anyone could, given the context, which is to say not at all, and opted to work with the material I've been given. And that ghost in my bedroom when I was a kid, the one I thought was my first? After a week or so, I finally told my mother about it. After all, she was the expert. She waited in my bedroom with me one night to see if the thing would appear. It did, and she recognized it right away: lights from passing cars outside, briefly filtering through the trees and shining on the wall at the foot of my bed.

A KNOCK ON THE DOOR
IN THE NIGHT

Someone knocked on our front door last night at a quarter to three. Adrift in the hazy borderlands of sleep, I bolted awake and lay still, fists clenched, listening. Would the knock come again, maybe harder this time? Would there be other sounds from outside—smashing windows, car alarms, shouting, sirens? Here in this tiny suburb of a tiny Cornish city, bored kids knock on doors at random hours and run. Because Although Cornwall is Britain's Florida, there's not much else for them to do. When tourist season ends and it's rainy and cold, a little merry thuggery livens things up. They go down to the pub, pound a few beers, pound on a few doors. In that blurry 3am state, I knew this already, I'd seen it in the news and the village Facebook group, and the knowledge meant nothing.

Hong Kong. Two and a half years after I escaped left that nightmare metropolis of tear gas and mass arrests and semi-random attacks by paramilitaries decked out in black, I can move through the day without scanning for threats. I can plan my routes the regular way: with satnav rather than social media and news updates. I don't check to see if I'm being followed. I'm okay now, more or less—a different okay. There's no rewinding the clock. I still wear black as a political act, and can't safely go back. The cops dragged people out of their homes at all hours, out of ambulances and emergency rooms, out of airport departure lounges. Grabbed bystanders off the sidewalks. They're still doing it.

There are knocks and there are knocks. There's the British kind that sounds like an apology rapped out against the wood: so sorry to disturb, it says. Would you happen to have a moment? There's the kind delivery drivers make: rushed and thunderous at times, a staccato born of long days behind the wheel of an Amazon van. Let's get this over with, it says. Eighteen more places to go today. Then there's the secret-police knock: sharp rather than loud, and with a tenor of malignance, authority gone wrong. It punches through the slumber of everyone inside. Eyes fly open, hearts race, palms film. It's part of our collective recollection. Kids will be kids, the villagers say on social media. So what if they've set a few park benches on fire, scared a few grannies, made noise after midnight. If they know they've made you angry, they'll keep at it. If they know they've scared you, even better. But we lived through hell a moment in history in a troubled corner of the world. In our old neighborhoods, the knocks on doors come not long before dawn.

Someone knocked on our door last night at a quarter to three. There are procedures for this, there are protocols: Check the lock. Look through a peephole. See who it is. Grab the baseball bat. Ask who's there. Ask Siri for help, or Alexa. Hit the panic button. Call the cops. Cops are for people who *can* call them, and cops will be cops, the Hong Kong government said. Just like boys will be boys. So what if they've set a few people on fire, killed a few grannies, and gassed half the city after midnight? As I move through the day, I scan for threats less now. I'm not *there* anymore. I'm just not sure I'm fully here either. At night before bed I look out the front window into the street and out the back one into the garden, hoping I won't see anyone in the shadows, watching. It takes longer to fall asleep now. I lie awake a lot, perfectly still, fists clenched, listening.

THE SCREWDRIVER
PEDAGOGIES

1.

I've just tripped over the tool kit. Since the door to my home office tends to drift shut, this black nylon satchel of utility sits on the floor propping it open. There's also nowhere else to put it. I bought the thing at B&Q, Britain's version of Home Depot. There's one down in Penryn, halfway to work, a big-box bonanza with aisles and aisles of objects and gadgets I've never known how to use but suspect I should own anyway. When I moved here from Hong Kong last year, I had an empty house, a furniture budget, and a certain gendered urge to be prepared for manual usefulness. Shelves to hang, flatpack furniture to assemble. In theory, I have everything I might need; in practice, there's very little I'll be able to use. Still, there's a comfort in having it.

2 .

My grandmother's gentleman friend owned a tract of land on the outskirts of New Bern, North Carolina. On it, he had his own trailer, plus a second one he rented to a local car salesman. Granny had her own place, a green and white mobile home with a redwood deck in the front almost the size of her living room. Just beyond the three trailers, toward the back of the property, a metal warehouse loomed. In the summer, it radiated heat, but once you slid open the massive front door and slipped inside, it was not cooler, exactly, but less sweltering.

Although we'd been warned not to play in there, it was a dusty wonderland of strange tools and machines. A car-restoration business leased out some of the space for a time. Hulks of old roadsters and sedans sat on racks silently awaiting reanimation. The mechanics puttered, took cigarette breaks, got back to puttering. The cars took on approximate shape but I never saw one completed. Look but don't touch, we were told.

Beyond that cavernous front space in the warehouse, there was another chamber, so to speak. Lower ceiling, dusty lights that barely pushed the dark back. It was a sculpture garden of filthy machines. Touch them and your fingers would come away black with unidentifiable grime. It should have been the perfect place for kids to play hide and seek, but the air stank of rust, old metal, and vague danger. It was a secret lair where thieves hid, an oubliette for objects and contraptions not touched in decades, a gateway I trespassed upon but never really passed through.

3.

I couldn't quite work out why we had to go to school. According to my mother, knowledge appeared in your head as you got older. She spoke French, or said she did, and had never studied it. It was just there. Don't worry, she reassured us. When you get older, you'll know how to speak it too, and you'll know how to cook and how to drive. In the same way, I believed the onset of adulthood would demystify the tools in the workshop downstairs. An understanding would coalesce in my brain like story ideas or useful tumors. I understood hammers, nails, and screwdrivers well enough. Pliers and drills and spirit levels. Chainsaws, soldering irons. My father didn't talk and my mother didn't stop, so in the version of reality she spun up for us, everything was mind over matter. We couldn't see the screws that held everything together. We just had to trust that they were there. Everything already existed, and if it didn't, it was about to. Case in point: Our house wasn't finished when we moved in. My father would retreat to his DIY warren in the basement, saw some wood, pound some nails, make some things. Like the old roadsters in the warehouse in New Bern, the house never seemed to be truly finished, only more *there* as the months turned into years. Cabinets, shelves, new carpets. I had nothing to do with it.

4.

I hated getting my hands dirty and my father hated that about me. The only thing worse than grease and grit on my fingers was the gelatinous crap we had to clean our hands with afterward. My father called it "Bappo" or something like that. It had the stiff, oily texture of petroleum jelly and smelled like a little pot of kerosene. The stains would go away but the stink would linger.

Prissy. Princess. Pristine. His disgust didn't toughen me up. I still detest getting my hands dirty.

5.

Amid all those gruff silences, there were a few father-son teaching moments:

* *Son, when you're sawing wood, you can't let the blade get bent. It won't go through clean.*
* *Son, when you hammer a nail, you've got to pound it right on the head. Drive it in.*
* *Son, steering a car is like steering a woman in bed. You've got to show her where to go.*

Or, to simplify: straightness. Anything bent is a problem.

6.

In college, my joints started to go. My left knee went first. I delivered pizzas for Domino's. When the regional manager showed up at our branch, we had to scramble. She'd yell "Good hustle! Good hustle!" if she was pleased with your performative rushing-about. If you weren't doing your part at helping Big Pizza reassure your starving fellow citizens that food could be summoned by people who were constantly dashing, she'd summon you to the back office for a stern word. The nights she wasn't there, which is to say most of them, there were often a few joints (the recreational kind) in circulation. I once melted a hole through the dashboard of the Domino's truck with one. And when my knee began feeling as if someone were hammering a nail through it, there was even more reason to augment reality with a puff or two before the next delivery. Or during. Or after.

Primed to ignore chronic pain until it settled in and carved its name on the mailbox out front, I pretended my hands didn't ache all the time until I couldn't anymore. I'd started working as an ASL interpreter, doing classes at my university as well as at the local community college. Overuse syndrome. Repetitive strain injuries. Carpal tunnel. For the next decade and a half, the pain in my hands, wrists, neck, and shoulders was a tidal force: sometimes debilitating, sometimes barely there at all. There were days I had to switch between ice baths and vats of hot water. Writing, while necessary in the same way oxygen is, didn't help. Hands poised over the keyboard, shoulders hunched, scowl of concentration: I wrecked my upper body, gobbling ibuprofen like Halloween candy to keep myself going. Bashed out my first novel. Lost feeling in a couple of fingers. Got it back.

Began thinking of a career change. Kept writing.

Back when my hands worked more reliably, when I had a modicum of grip strength, I could have learned tools, wiring, houses. I could have learned to install a window before one closed.

7.

I can identify maybe ⅔ of the tools in the kit. More than half, certainly. There's a measuring tape, an assortment of screwdrivers, and a hammer or two. Pliers, wrenches, and a wire cutter so sharp I left it in its protective plastic packaging to protect my fingers. There's a metal file of some sort—is it an awl, an asp, a rasp?—and a level. I'd list the other ones but I'd have to take them out and check online to know what they're called. In theory, all this male cutlery ought to help me bash my way through most household contingencies. In practice, I'll text the landlord and let him sort it out. Or I'll text the handyman I hired to assemble the furniture and hang shelves I could trust not to pitch forward off their mountings and crash to the floor. Either way, they'll both arrive with their own sets of tools.

8.

If the stereotype holds, men from Generation X invented the Internet but can't change a tire. Our fathers were missing but there, there but missing. They wanted to say goodbye to a part of themselves,

I suspect, in the same way some immigrants don't teach their children their homeland's language. They wanted to raise a tribe of soft-handed bosses in offices, not the guys on the factory floor. It would prove something had been achieved. It would also be a perpetual defeat, ensuring they'd continue being needed.

I'm writing about a loss that may not be a loss, about an observation with faint tasting notes of blame. Manhood isn't bashing your way through life, pounding nails and children and women, keeping them straight. It took moving away from North Carolina to learn that. Before then, I worried a lot. I seemed to be terrible at manning. I know better now, but I'd like to be handier. I'd also like hands that more or less work. In the meantime, the tool kit sits at the ready, guarding the door, comforting me.

STORMS AND BOXES

Fall 2020, Truro

I've just moved into a newly renovated terrace house in the outskirts of Truro, down in Cornwall, starting mostly from scratch. Everything, husband and cat included, is back in Hong Kong. Too busy and distracted to follow the news, I've been assembling flatpack furniture and setting up the TV. There's enough cardboard to build a sturdy garden shed if not an actual house. When the recycling guys came by yesterday morning, I hauled it all that packaging out to the curb. They took some of it but not all. Two of the boxes were just too big.

"Mate, I'd lose my job if I took that," one of the crew explains. "It would fill up the compartment for card, and we wouldn't be able to finish our route. We'd get the sack."

"Oh. Sorry, I didn't know. Am I supposed to take it to the tip then?"

I'm American. Southern. We don't talk like this. The "tip" is the dump. We use more commas when we talk. I at least do know where the tips are. There's one down near Penryn. Supposedly one here in Truro too, on the other side of the city. But because we're in the middle of the Covid pandemic, I don't know if they're open. The viral apocalypse has abated a bit, just not enough that any semblance of normal life has come back.

"Call the council. They've got a big van for pickups like this. They'll send someone round."

So I'm left with two big boxes full of bits and pieces of cardboard: fragments of smaller boxes I've torn apart, those hollow pyramids that protect the corners of new furniture, various rectangles and inserts. My little front lawn's wet from recent rain, so in my vast brilliance I decide to leave the boxes in place. After all, it would make a mess of the carpets to drag them back through the house into the conservatory. Besides, the council's going to send someone round.

I do manage to get someone on the phone. Vague promises are made. Then the storm hits.

Having lived in Hong Kong more than a decade, I'm familiar with typhoons. Went through a few strong ones there. A couple would have been classified as category 4 hurricanes in North America. One was a category 5, although I think it weakened just before it hit. Since Hong Kong's engineered to withstand a direct hit from the kind of major storm that would flatten an American city—but not sturdy enough to withstand democracy, it would seem—I got used to kind of ignoring them. Now and then they got scary. The windows would flex, or leak. Sometimes water would blow in through the air-conditioning units. The building might sway. But the power stayed on. The water was usually fine, although I'd buy bottles just in case. And we had a good filter on the tap. Here, well, somehow I didn't realize that these Atlantic storms would blow in and deliver the same kind of pounding.

The rain starts late in the afternoon: steady, then harder, becoming a sustained downpour. *Oh shit—the boxes.* The tops are open. They're full. All that cardboard, now wet, plus whatever water has gotten inside. The downpour is the kind of torrent that would be categorized as red rainfall or black in Hong Kong. When the Hong Kong Observatory issues a black rain warning, you shelter in place. Schools and offices close, or you stay home until it subsides. This is the kind of intense pissing-down rarely seen outside of the tropics, a relentless thunder against the polycarbonate roof of my conservatory.

Now the wind is screaming, the same howl against the windows that so unnerved me in Hong Kong. I live in a mid-terrace house in a suburban neighborhood. The stronger gusts send shockwaves through the whole structure. If I was going to drag those sodden boxes inside, the window for that has just closed. Steeling myself, I dash out into the storm and push them up against the privet hedge to shelter them from the worst of the wind. As expected, they're soggy already. The top flaps bang open and shut, although the cardboard detritus inside has so far stayed put, too waterlogged to take flight.

Outside, the wind doesn't feel as strong as it sounds. Fall is here, and the tree at the north end of the terrace has dropped most of its leaves. Its naked branches amplify the howling. Encouraged by this, I shove the two huge boxes as close to the hedge as I can, the tamp the stuff inside down to pack it tight. They're heavy now, too much so to go airborne. And the wind isn't that strong... or is it?

Although you can't predict exactly what a typhoon will do, there are patterns. You pay attention to the bands. The first rains hit. They sting. Is it because the droplets are smaller or the winds are stronger? Maybe both? In Hong Kong, even if you haven't seen the alerts that get posted everywhere a day or two before a typhoon hits, you can tell one is coming. The storm system blocks the pollution and haze the prevailing winds normally blow out to sea. The air grows heavy and dense, filthy. There's no wind, and the pressure-cooker humidity is unbearable. When the outer bands pass over, it's a blessing. They're like a giant broom. You can breathe again. It gets cooler.

The typhoon bears down in a way that is tidal, inexorable. Those fine, slashing showers give way to much heavier ones. There's a tension in the air. You ask yourself is this your own nerves twanging in anticipation of dangers to come? Or is it something external, some yet-unquantified characteristic of an incoming storm? With the preliminary Signal 1 warning, you will have started keeping an eye on the news. Every channel shows the warning symbols on the corner of the broadcast screen while they are in effect. There will be a sign up in the lobby of every office tower or apartment block you enter. Next up is Signal 3. The storm is closer. The winds are stronger, the rains are heavier. It still might not make a direct hit, but the city's in for a few days of intense weather. Signal 8 is the one that shuts the city down. Schools and offices close. Trading on the Hang Seng stock exchange halts. You either go home or stay put. There might still be time to nip down to the supermarket around the corner but you keep an eye on the rainfall just in case. Wind speeds at signal 8 are comparable to those of a tropical storm on the Safir - Simpson Scale. There's a signal 9, but I don't know what it's for. Signal 10 is "holy fuck, Batman." That's what this one sounds like.

Now and then, the wind relents for a few minutes, then picks up again. In the worst moments of bellowing, I go to the windows and look outside. Have those sodden boxes exploded yet? In my head, a horror movie plays on a loop. The wind intensifies. The boxes disintegrate, showering the cul de sac with bits and shreds of cardboard litter. By this time, I've finally had sense enough to check the weather online. Although *The Guardian* is weirdly silent on meteorological issues, *Cornwall Live* has little else to talk about. Oh, it's one of those storms *with names.* These things blow in and make a mess of everything. I had no idea one was coming, much less how bad it would be. I left two cardboard boxes out in it. I'm in for a long night.

Summer 2019, Hong Kong

Another week, another million-person march. There's a sense of determination in the air. It's mixed with disbelief. How could Carrie Lam, the city's Chief Executive, possibly have been so stupid as to introduce that bill that would have permitted extradition up to China, and so obdurate as to double down and refuse to withdraw it? Did half a million people not take to the streets when a similar bill was proposed during a previous administration? There have already been several huge marches, urban rivers of black-clad people making their—our—way from Victoria Park in Causeway Bay over to the new government complex on the waterfront at Tamar. This bill will be a disaster if it passes. Hong Kong's success in trade and finance stems from its together-but-apart status with China. It's a gateway, an entrepôt, but—and this is key—there's no extradition agreement with the mainland. No one other than Lam seems to want one.

It's already been a long day. We cabbed over to Causeway Bay from my home just across the harbor around noon. Quick lunch at a *cha chaan teng*—Hong Kong's homegrown version of a fast-food restaurant, with an extensive menu and quick but gruff service—and then we joined the crowd. The sun glares down; the streets would be shimmery with rising heat if we could see them for all the people. We've got bottled water in our backpacks. Caps and sunscreen. Handheld electric fans. Everyone around us is in black to signify solemnity and grief. To an extent, each march is a funeral procession. It's a widespread view that Hong Kong is dying. There's nothing to celebrate. Everyone is calm, resolved, polite, anxious.

The official route ends near the Pacific Place shopping/office/residential complex in Admiralty, near the government buildings. The crowd parts: some head for the mall—there are restrooms, polar air conditioning, and an MTR station underneath—and others veer right, toward Tamar. We're curious. Something's happening over there.

As we approach, we begin to see people in masks and bandanas approaching marchers and gesturing not to take photos. Don't capture anyone's face, they caution us. And be quiet. Signs saying the same thing have been printed out on A4 paper and taped to every wall in sight. Enough has already happened this summer. We all know what the stakes are.

The crowd around the Legislative Council building is bigger than we expect.

THUD.

Cheers.

"What the hell?"

We wend our way through the thickening rowd to get a closer look. Everyone is oddly silent, talking in hushed tones. Many are wearing sunglasses, caps, blue surgical masks.

THUD.

More cheers.

We exchange puzzled looks. A few moments later, we've got a view of the building's main entrance. At first we can't tell what's going on. The flags of Hong Kong and China have been taken down; in their place flies the black bauhinia, the protest flag created sometime

44

earlier in the summer when the HKSAR government's recalcitrance became clear. The frontliners—the most hardcore protestors, the ones who have already scuffled with the police after previous marches—have assembled a crude battering ram out of a shopping cart.

"Holy shit, they're not really going to..."

THUD.

Yes, they are. They're bashing their way into LegCo.

"This is not going to end well," I say, still incredulous. "We need to get the fuck out of here."

And we do. Is this the moment when things in Hong Kong turned dark? From my vantage point here in Truro, I think not. It's a frightening night, to be sure, but the fear comes from anticipation. At home, we're glued to the TV, or I am. My partner makes dinner. On Facebook, I post a message asking friends to watch the news, to bear witness. I'm certain the police will attack. They already have, after previous marches. But not this time.

No, for me the moment when Hong Kong's protest season truly turns scary comes on July 21. A mob of gangsters bashes their way into a suburban MTR station, boards the train, and beats the shit out of the passengers. It's on the news that night shortly after it happens. The video is the stuff of nightmares: white-shirted thugs waling on cowering people—women, kids, elderly people—unlucky enough to be in the wrong place at the wrong time. The randomness of this, the sheer insanity—I can't get my head around it. No one can. I'm shouting "WHAT THE FUCK? WHAT THE FUCK?" at the TV. We're both crying. This is personal, too. That used to be my station. I lived up there for two years and still pass through on my way to and from work. That could have been me, or my partner.

We keep seeing it, over and over in a hellish loop on social media and the news. Men in white shirts chasing terrified commuters. People begging for their lives and getting beaten down with truncheons and rods of some sort. The police are nowhere to be found. I suspect our disbelief matches that of the victims: *This couldn't happen here. This can't be happening here. This is not supposed to happen here.* Hong Kong is, or was, one of the safest and most orderly places on Earth. People keep to themselves and get on with it. A certain gruff live-and-let-live ethos prevails. Why stir up trouble when you could be monitoring your investments, opening a shop, or buying another flat for your property portfolio?

"And it *would* have been you," confirms a friend who used to be in the triads. He has the experience and connections to know which gang the thugs belong to and who hired them. "You'd be a target up there. Just because you're white. If you'd been on that train, they'd have killed you." This part never makes the news. Here's a tidbit Reuters and the rest of the networks never learn: the attack was meant as a warning. Anger at the protestors for scaring mainland tourists away. Businesses up in those border communities have been losing money. Somehow the US is blamed for instigating the protests as well, a narrative I'm sure we haven't heard the last of.

Fall 2020, Truro

Wind batters the house. The walls flex. I'm pretty sure the roof will stay on, but the fact that "pretty sure" is the most confidence I can muster is part of what's keeping me up. The rain is machine-gun fire on the conservatory roof just under my bedroom window. Every time I think I'm about to doze off, the storm intensifies. It's ridiculous. I don't know how I could have moved to a place with extreme weather like this and not known. It's the kind of thing I would know. Should know. When the howling outside reaches a certain pitch, I trudge to my home office to look outside. The two boxes sway like fat ballerinas in leg irons. I know they're too waterlogged to go anywhere but that image of an explosion of cardboard won't stop dogging me. How could I not have known about this? What on earth made me think it was a good idea to leave boxes outdoors? So what if I'd dragged a soggy cardboard mess across the carpets? They would *dry*. I have *towels*. That's one of my quirks: I always have more towels than I'll ever need. You never know when you'll need towels. I like buying them. Besides, I'm alone here. There's no one else around to complain.

I used to be better at thinking. Permanent Head Damage: that's the joke a couple of my friends tell about PhDs. Before I started mine, I scoffed. Then I finished, and understood. Then came the protests, months after months of intensifying violence amid a backdrop of relentless government gaslighting. Then the pandemic started. Then I got this job and moved to England, leaving my partner (now husband) and cat back in Hong Kong. It's taken a toll. On my way back to bed, I go to the bathroom again. Might as well take a leak so I won't have to lie under the covers trying to determine whether there's enough in my bladder to bother getting up again and emptying it. The kind of thinking I do at this time of night: it's not like it used to be. This is England. I'm not supposed to feel helpless here. When I moved to Korea in 2005, I often felt helpless. The whole three years I was there, I felt helpless. My heating-oil tank ran dry on a subzero night because no one had explained how the system worked, what the panel on the wall of my apartment was for. That afternoon, I got home and noticed a red light had come on. Was it on before? I wasn't sure. It was frigid out. My next-door neighbor, a Chinese guy from Shanghai who also taught at my university, had student helpers. I didn't. They figured it out. The elderly couple who ran the convenience store across the street helped me order a refill. Somehow I figured out how to say that in Korean. Things work differently there, and there's that complicated language with its knotty, crocheted grammar. I put a space heater in the bedroom and hoped I'd wake up. As an American in the UK, I thought I'd have an easier time getting things done.

For the rest of the night, I'm in and out of bed like a parent with a newborn. Wails wake me up from the syrupy doze I drift into now and then. I might sleep an hour at a time, maybe two. The storm still hasn't blown over. Even if wind speeds in some of those typhoons back in Hong Kong were higher, this is relentless. Hours and hours of it. The walls creak. Rain smacks the windows like gravel pellets. When it gets really loud, I go back to the office, look outside. I go down to the kitchen once for a closer look. The boxes are right there, maybe eight feet from the window. On closer inspection, one of them is warping. It's longer and narrower than the other, now losing its shape, slumping in the middle.

Eventually I do manage to fall asleep, a real sleep this time. The storm is still raging but less intensely now. I'm not sure how many hours I get. Checking the time on my phone is depressing. How long have I been in this awful cycle of tossing, turning, nodding off, waking up, and looking outside? And why can I not take my own word for it that the boxes aren't going to blow up? Maybe it's that last big typhoon, the category 5 one. That one was bad. The wind woke me up around nine. My husband was still asleep. I got up, made coffee, fed the cat. That apartment had big picture windows with views of

48

an open area in Hung Hom, a few buildings, and beyond them, the harbor. The palm trees next to the pool down below—I was on the 15th floor—were already taking a lashing. As the morning wore on, the weather deteriorated fast. The racket outside was a jet-engine scream at times. Around lunchtime, the stronger gusts would make those big windows flex. If they broke, it would be a disaster: I didn't have anything to put up as a barrier, and we'd have to grab the cat and flee, maybe riding the storm out in the lobby downstairs. Was it too late to tape big Xs over the windows?

"Please don't break," I begged the glass, almost praying. "Please don't break. Please don't break. Please don't break."

I washed a Xanax down with my second cup of coffee.

People started posting videos of the damage on social media. A crane atop one of those skyscrapers came loose and fell. The wind tore the facade completely off an older building in some distant district. In a waterfront housing estate on the eastern edge of the island, waves seven stories high hit the building closest to the harbor, smashing windows and flooding the parking garage in the basement. A Maserati drowned. So did its owner. There was water knee-deep in hotels and offices, and windows all along the harbor blew out. Stacks of paperwork on desks were sucked out into the vortex, blown out to sea. Trees came down all over campus at the university where I worked. One was leaning alarmingly against the library building. Others landed in a heap on the roof of a covered walkway. The sound of chainsaws faded into the background roar of the city.

I recall being hardier once, more resilient. Here in England I've discovered a new form of crying. It requires a pillow. At some point the sobs turn so hard and desperate my whole body convulses. The sobs become screams. I need the pillow to muffle them. At some point they subside and become rattles, hitches, and the occasional gasp for air. My throat will ache, as will my jaws. Since leaving Hong Kong, I have been doing quite a lot of this.

The morning is calmer. The rain lets up now and then. Now and then it's torrential, but there are calm spells too. There are a couple of home-improvement stores a short drive away: The Range and Homebase. By this point I've decided I need some kind of durable, all-weather duct tape to wrap around the boxes, to make sure they hold together. We're not out of the woods yet. According to the Met Office, it'll be another day or so before the storms blow themselves out. After that, there'll be rain. It would now be almost impossible to haul the boxes back inside, and while I'm less worried about the wind pulverizing them and festooning the neighborhood with my trash, I'm still gay and Southern enough to deplore messes and ick on the lawn, hedge or no hedge.

At The Range, I find sturdy-looking tape. The packaging says that it's waterproof. I buy a couple of rolls, pick up random other shit I may need someday (when you're furnishing a house from zero-na-da-scratch, there's always something else you've realized you haven't bought yet), head back home. Now it's pouring again. No, now the sun's out. No, now the sun's out *and* it's pouring. Must be a Cornwall thing. I park, hurry inside, open up one package of supertape, dash back outside, and… the adhesive won't stick to wet cardboard. Nor to itself. Seems it has to be dry to work. Then it can get wet. I recall that saying about the definition of insanity: repeating the same action in hopes or expectations of a different result. Having somehow become a person who screams into bedding, I can sort of accept this.

Fall 2019, Hong Kong

We're having a quiet typhoon season so far, and we're not. There's one tropical storm, a weak signal 8. High winds push rain through the bay window ledge into our bedroom. We've just moved into a comfortable flat in the lower Mid-Levels. I'm the first to notice the water collecting underneath the paint. It bulges: ugly little pouches like frogs' bellies. These swell as the storm rages mildly outside. It's far from the worst one we've been through, more of a messy annoyance. There are enough calm moments that I can dash down to the convenience store around the corner for soft drinks and snacks without getting soaked or knocked down. When the wind and rain pick up again, more water comes through. On closer inspection, there's water inside the marble slab of the ledge. It's also coming through the windows in the living room. Shoddy construction. We text the landlords.

Nothing about the season is quiet, though. Every weekend brings fresh violence. The protests take place weekly, sometimes more often, and end in urban warfare. The whole city is engulfed in tear gas at times. We're high enough uphill that the fumes won't reach our street but we have to be careful going out. Before I walk down to the gym, I check Twitter to make sure the route is safe. Between sets, I keep checking. Several times, I have to cut a workout short because the cops are gassing Central. If I take a taxi home, the route will take us west, away from the spiralling violence, before turning to go up the hill. But if I'm walking, I usually take the escalator back. It's not the most direct route, but the way home is steep and even on good days my knees ache like two broken light bulbs trying to fuck. Most of the time, it's safe to walk the few blocks back to the escalator access platform on Queens Road Central. But even three more blocks, there are often barricades on Pedder Street and D'Aguilar. The cops are in all-black combat gear with their warrant cards hidden and reflective tape over their visors. Everyone knows mainland paramilitaries are embedded with them even though the government keeps denying it. Now and then someone gets hauled away, right off the sidewalk.

The universities are bombs with long fuses lit and getting shorter. Practically everyone—even the mainlanders, or so I'm told in the strictest of confidence—supports the democratic cause. Whether or not they show up for class, most students wear protest black now. Black bloc is the new semiformal. Many are frontliners. Demonstrations occur almost daily. It has been noticed I wear black every day now as well. Remarks have been made. I'm fine with that; I want to be clear where my allegiances are. I'm not alone, either: I've spotted colleagues in the marches.

We keep thinking we've seen the worst. One Friday afternoon, we're notified to dismiss class early. Weekends are generally bad. Tonight will be worse. The MTR is going to shut down. One boy from Shenzhen begs me to let him go right away. He's going straight home. His eyes are huge, he's welling up with tears, and his voice is shaking.

"Go," I tell him.

Fuck it, I wrap up then and there. I've got a long hike home from my campus in Tuen Mun, a suburban area in Hong Kong's northwest borderlands. There will be a protest right at Central Station when I arrive. I'll have no choice but to go through it. It's not the protestors I'm worried about, it's the cops. Might as well get started before it gets too bad. The students wish me good luck and tell me to be safe; I say the same to them.

When I get there, the station's closing down. Only one or two entrances remain open. Workers from Central are heading home in droves, the kind of crowds you see in an evacuation, which is what this is, when you think about it. Offices are shutting down. The anxiety is palpable. I have to exit at street level instead of going through the IFC shopping mall—which is closing and barricading its doors—as usual; there are massive crowds outside, and more barricades, and legions of Hong Kong's hypermilitarized and out-of-control police.

Some of my students have vanished. I put one foot in front of the other. There are rumors of gang rapes up in one of the detention centers on the border. Young men as well as young women. I've been told the arrests are made based not on criteria of legality but fuckability. Certain age groups are prioritized. I know people who would know. One of my students told me his boyfriend got arrested. He camped out outside the police station in [name of district redacted] all weekend until he—the boyfriend—was released. Unraped, evidently. I've also read there are special trains for the arrested. They're transported up to China. Not all of them come back.

I make my way through the crowd, many of whom are in black bloc. Stop to give cover to someone spray-painting graffiti onto the road. Marks & Spencer has already closed, and the one halfway up the hill will probably also be shutting its doors pretty soon. So much for what I planned to cook for dinner.

This will turn out to be my last time on campus for the rest of the term. The weekend is as bad as expected: clashes, scuffles, round-ups, mass arrests. People are fleeing by boat to Taiwan. It's not that far. An underground network of activists helps to arrange it.

The cops have two water cannon vehicles, and both are in use. The water contains blue dye and something painful. They won't tell the hospitals what the ingredients are.

Friday is bad. Monday is worse. Protestors shut down the MTR during the morning commute. Things get bad fast in Central. I cancel my morning class and get in trouble for it. My department head threatens to give me a warning letter. After a weekend of horror and rage, I'm amazed there's anything new to feel. I'd like to set him on fire.

The cops attack the universities. It's a war zone up at Chinese University of Hong Kong. Archers. Overland supply routes to the students who have barricaded themselves in. I know some of the drivers. Even the university president gets gassed in his efforts to intervene. Soon thereafter, PolyU makes the news and stays there. It's encircled. Things go from bad to worse to blazing hellfire very, very fast.

Classes are cancelled: first day by day, then a week at a time, then for good. The international students and the mainlanders are evacuated. One girl from the mainland is overlooked, left behind, and she despairs when Beijing boasts it has rescued all of its students from lawless Hong Kong. They haven't. She is livid, appalled, suicidal. I call and arrange an intervention. My students are still my students, wherever they're from, and I've been told again and again that the mainland kids can see through all this. They can't speak up, but they know exactly what's going on. I wouldn't call them allies, not exactly, but they are hopeful things will get better in China someday.

Finally, another storm does blow through. Signal 3 this time, not a direct hit, just enough wind and rain to wash the gas and screaming out of the air. There's a pause, one we've needed.

Fall 2020, Truro

It's clear the council is never going to pick up the the cardboard. The storm has mostly blown over. Intermittent rain trails in its wake. The boxes have now been out in the banshee winds for three days. Either I do something about this or they will stay there until they merge with the earth. Cardboard under such conditions sort of congeals. Objectively speaking, there's nothing difficult about this. I've already managed to buy a car and rent a house. Hell, I managed to get a job in the UK and a work visa during the pandemic. Leaving two big cardboard boxes out in a windstorm should not be this traumatic, except it is. I haven't gotten more than about two hours' sleep at a stretch this weekend.

Google's not helping. Although there has to be someone I can hire to come over in a truck and cart this shit away to wherever you take it here for disposal, my Internet searches keep giving pages of semi-relevant but useless results. Industrial-waste removers. Construction-site cleanup. Disinfection. Hell, I find folks who'll come in and clean up the stains after Grandma dies. Just not this.

I keep thinking the neighbors are going to say something. Although I haven't spoken to them yet, haven't met them, I imagine myself surrounded by a star-spangled aura of postcolonial incompetence. The other residents of this terrace are peeping out the windows at me, taking pictures, and posting them on Instagram with slogans like "MOVED TO ENGLAND. GETTING IT WRONG." Or just #yankfailure with a Union Jack emoji. Of course this is not actually happening, but I have the same paranoid imaginings behind the wheel. I drive far too slowly up and down these narrow Cornish rat runs. Even the comparatively benign A39 between Truro and

Falmouth scares me at times. It's twisty. There are hedgerows alongside it most of the way, not broad American shoulders where sudden contingencies can be safely addressed. Here, you have to hope you can limp to the next layby. Drivers behind me must think they're following pensioners. I'm only 50.

Like a bolt of bad figurative language from out of the blue, I finally find what I'm looking for: a company that specializes in more conventional forms of waste disposal. There's a "man with a van" plan. Not exactly cheap—it'll cost about £110—but at this point I'm almost ready to hand a stranger my credit card and throw in a blowjob for good measure. Two days later, I get home from work to find the boxes gone. Later that same afternoon, a cheerful guy in a uniform knocks on my door. He's there for the rest of the shit that I have to get rid of. It takes him less than ten minutes to haul away the pile of empty furniture boxes in my conservatory. All that cardboard, all those Styrofoam protective wedges, all those tangles of plastic cables—all gone. The sudden empty space improves the quality of the silences. Whisper-echoes of my footsteps across the tiles of the conservatory. A resonant hush from the carpets in the den. It's raining again and the sun's out, but that's the default here. For the first time in days, I can look outside from my office window and see all the way to the horizon. I've dealt with the first of the boxes, but there will be others.

ON SURVEILLANCE

1.

It began with a back-of-mind whisper eight or nine years ago, sus-
picion giving way to awareness: *I might be under surveillance.* I lived
in Hong Kong then. Edward Snowden had holed up in the Mira
Hotel a few blocks down the street from my apartment. I felt bad for
the guy. I fled the US once, albeit on my own terms and without the
intelligence community in pursuit. History has a habit of proving
whistleblowers right. In the meantime, while you wait for the details
to emerge, you still have to buy groceries. So on Twitter, I offered. It
was not a political act. You just can't live on convenience-store ramen
and room service forever. This might not have been my brightest
moment, I'll admit. He didn't reply, and subsequently went into hiding. After that, I wondered: *Did I just put a bullseye on my back?*

2.

I have a rather large head. If you've ever been to Australia, you might have seen the mannequins in clothing stores. The bodies are more or less human. Huge cartoon-like manga heads sit atop them. Think Betty Boop; think Peanuts. They're grotesque. Although mine is not *that* out of proportion, it seems bigger than most. Hats are tight. So are glasses. When I moved to Britain in 2020, this presented certain problems. Apart from a few kitchen items I thought I'd need upon arrival—my French press and my favorite coffee mug, among other things—I had to furnish my whole house from scratch. Here's a thing I learned: metal colanders are not common here, especially if you want the kind with a handle. There are plastic ones. Also mesh, but one of those would be more like a yarmulke than the helmet I need. I can improvise. Aluminium foil, as it's spelled here, should do the trick. The sparkly colander crinkles when I put it on, but at least it fits over my head. It disrupts the panopticon. Skynet can't see me. Can the neighbors?

3.

Everybody knows who *they* are: the whispering faceless people who are invisible and everywhere and can do things, the villagers with their rumors and torches and power tools. Lyrics are written about them. These grey sideliners can destroy relationships, cast the innocent into abjection, ruin lives. They're also good at infrastructure. *They're* building a new road, a new bridge, a new shopping center. *They say* creeps into conversation daily. *They* creep. But who are *they*, exactly? Neighbors you catch glimpses of. Students taking classes other than your own. People you pass on the sidewalk. Agents of enemy states. Do they turn their heads as you walk by? Photograph you, or murmur voice notes into their phones? Fill out reports when they get home? Send faxes? In the interest of not letting *them* see me in my new house, I bought the thickest light-blocking curtains I could find at Dunelm. I was hoping to find some that might block out X-rays and satellite transmissions, but no such luck. They just block out the sun. My bedroom faces east. On those rare mornings when the sky isn't a solid pall of low clouds, sunrise can be a bit much. The light creeps in anyway. There's a great deal of creeping.

4.

As a child, I was under constant surveillance—the extrasensory kind. My mother claimed she was a powerful clairvoyant. She kept telepathic tabs on my sister and me throughout the day. She always knew where we were, what we were doing, what we were thinking. The world had become so jaded and dangerous, she thought it best to keep us as safe and innocent as possible. We'd have better child-hoods that way. Happier ones. To that end, she'd remind us she could see us at all times. I'd ask, even in the bathroom? She'd reply, I gave birth to you and changed your diapers. She'd tell stories of her fabulous psychic exploits: how she could read our father's thoughts, how she could tell when we were upset, how she could predict the future. As the years passed, I worked to fabricate a barrier around my mind so that no one could get in. I now verge on invisible. Most people emit a faint "I'm here" signal but I don't; I have no presence at all in most rooms unless I choose to turn it on, which is exhausting.

This is annoying at bars and restaurants when I need service. I might not need that colander.

5.

Once upon a time in France, motorists would spray a thick coat of hairspray on their license plates in an attempt to fool speed cameras. When the stuff dried, it would form a reflective surface—a translucent balaclava. I thought about trying it out myself but when I lived on the West Coast, everyone sped. No need to put AquaNet on my Honda. Once upon a time in Singapore, a friend told me there were hidden CCTV cameras everywhere. Security agents with binoculars stationed in surrounding shopping malls and office buildings, scanning for scofflaws and troublemakers. Gum-chewers, jaywalkers, graffiti taggers. Even the attendants in public restrooms would harangue you if you forgot to flush the toilet. Order *uber alles*. I was careful not to jaywalk. Once upon a time in Hong Kong, I corrected a student when he said Taiwan and meant Taipei: "But Taiwan is the *country*, not the city!" The four girls from mainland China in that class gasped in unison. In China, there's always a Party monitor in every university classroom, spying on the lecturer. That wasn't the case in Hong Kong when I lived there. Or was it? I spent the next couple of weeks anxious I'd get sacked.

6.

After the 2014 protests in Hong Kong, I began to wonder if my Internet activity was being monitored. I ticked several "troublesome foreigner" boxes: writer, publisher, academic, American, active on social media, gay. The night the protests kicked off, I was out there. I didn't get tear-gassed—not then, anyway—but could smell and feel the stinging dregs of it hanging in the air. Like many in that well-educated, hyperconnected city, I gave little thought to the traces my reportage might leave. Threads on Twitter. Rants on Facebook. I think I still had a blog then. I was careful online: aggressive ad blockers, tracking blockers, script blockers, you name it. At some point I got a VPN. In fact, I got two: one for personal use and another my university furnished for work trips to China. I can't say when my suspicions gave way to actual concern. Finances and porn: that's what it boiled down to. I didn't want anyone to see how much or how little I had in the bank and where I kept it. And the rest: well, you get the idea. How much or how little. Where I wanted it put. I covered the webcam on my laptop with a slip of folded paper. It's still there. The show's over.

7.

In late 2015, five members of the staff of Causeway Bay Books, a bookstore that specialized in books on political topics that could not be published in China, were kidnapped by some mysterious *they*.

They detained three while on visits to the mainland, nabbed the fourth at his home in Hong Kong, and renditioned the last from his residence in Thailand. It seemed the books had rankled senior government officials in Beijing. Ergo, the store and its staff had to vanish, despite not having broken any laws. When you're in detention in China, the surveillance is constant, oppressive, or so I've been told. Your jailers watch you 24/7, even while you're sleeping or taking a shit. They bark questions. There are cameras. To keep you from committing suicide, you're given a toothbrush tied to a string. If you try to choke yourself with it, your captors will yank it out of your mouth. In the interest of not being arrested, my business partner at the press and I dropped one China-related book from our list and paused sales of another by a Hong Kong author who'd been deemed politically problematic. We were not kidnapped, but made sense to assume *they* were watching.

8.

During the 2019 protests in Hong Kong, I had to proceed as if my Internet activity was being monitored. I ticked the same "troublesome foreigner" boxes plus a couple of new ones: participant in multiple marches, known associate of high-profile activists, strident on social media. In the first protests that year, people were less concerned, less afraid. It was Hong Kong, after all. Protests were part of the culture there. People felt safe, until suddenly we weren't. As the violence intensified, week after week, month after month, covering your face became standard procedure. Baseball cap, sunglasses, surgical mask. The march organizers knew where CCTV cameras had been installed. At critical points, people would be stationed to warn marchers to hide their faces. Sometimes they'd hand out surgical masks if they had any. But: I'm white and my arms are tattooed. Not hard to identify. Also, there were infiltrators. And as the protests wore on and the government dug in its heels and gassed the whole city, new questions arose. Black-clad citizens tore down one new "smart camera" that the government insisted wasn't meant for surveillance. No more were put up, but it triggered a mass decision to go dark on social media. I deleted my Twitter accounts and locked down my postings on Facebook. Deleted photos, stopped blogging, switched to encrypted apps, hid behind the VPN, frantically looked for jobs elsewhere. Even in English, there were codes, slang, vernacular work-arounds when discussing protest-related topics. You never knew who was listening, who was watching. Safer to assume you were not safe. Because in Hong Kong, *they* were more than just lazy linguistic placeholders.

9.

Surveillance shapes your life when you grow up in a small town. Someone's always watching: the neighbors, random passersby, fellow students. They behave like agents of enemy states, starting whisper campaigns, spreading rumors. The effect is more profound when you're gay and in the South or somewhere like it. Therefore, you self-monitor: your gait, your voice, your gestures, your clothes. Does your ass swing when you walk. Do you exaggerate certain syllables. Do your wrists go a bit limp now and then. Don't wear pink. Expect to get hurt. A walk down the street to a shop can result in your face being slammed against the sidewalk, or worse. You're well acquainted with the dripping itch of spit as it runs down your cheek. If you're well-enough known or just obvious, no one will help. And yet, the surveillance also includes the few souls who aren't like that, who might intervene. The surveillance takes place because of everything about you and nothing you've chosen to be. What is authentic and what is performance? It doesn't matter. Nothing exists but the relentlessness. If you want to live, you grow armor.

10.

I'm old enough to remember the advent of motion-sensing urinals. You stood in front of the electric eye as we called it then, did your business, and stepped away. It would flush automatically. Of course I was paranoid. Psychic monitoring was one thing. I didn't have to see the equipment. But I didn't want the leering creep on the other side of the electric eye to see *my* equipment. It's all right, my parents assured me. There's nobody there, it's not a camera, it's just a machine. No one can see you. As much as I wanted to believe them, I started using bathroom stalls whenever I could. When I got older, I began to care less. I understood the technology, for one thing, and besides: if someone wanted to see my junk that badly, let them look. Consent is not the antidote to surveillance, defiance under a façade of discretion is. I learned that lesson on sidewalks and in public restrooms as a boy. There has always been a bullseye on my back. I do not consent. I have never consented.

THE DEPARTURE BOARD

Seattle

My lawyer's talking about blowjobs. I found him via an ad in Seattle's gay weekly. To an extent, I welcome the blue-tinged banter. Although he has issues with boundaries, at least I don't have to worry about homophobia. I'm breaking messily up with a man. I've been supporting him. This is complicated and it is unpleasant. The tech crash after 9/11 cut my income in half, I was a shattered empty vessel after an earlier breakup with someone I was supposed to get old with, and this rebound I met in the East Village at The Cock the night before flying to Amsterdam for reasons that are murky now moved from Brooklyn to Oakland to live with me after four months and is prone to fits of screaming. Not all surprises are good. Now I've come to some semblance of... perhaps not sanity, exactly, but stasis. The lawyer—we'll call him Greg—is here to help with the disentanglement. I scheduled half an hour for the appointment but I've been here almost twice that. All my paperwork's in order, but the story about some guy whose cock he sucked has gone on much longer than the act itself did. But if I go home, there will be ranting and shouting. Given the choice between my attorney's naked escapades and my partner's mostly fictional but very loud indignities, the vicarious sword-swallowing is a great deal less tiresome.

I have never liked being a captive audience. In childhood, I often was. Some quality makes me attractive to people who rant. My mother did, in the car, driving, often relentlessly. I was there to be a sympathetic spittoon for her sorrows. Overflowing, I became obsessed with faking my own death. You had to be careful with that kind of thing, though. No one wants to wake up halfway through their own autopsy. Characters in the novels I read would go to City Hall, find a birth certificate for a baby born around the same time as themselves but which then died in infancy, steal the certificate, and use it to set up a new identity in some other city. With just that piece of ID, you could then open a bank account, get a driver's license, anything you needed. You could vanish. Provided you moved to some distant part of the country, no one would know. No one would find you. It would take more money than I had, though, and more time. Besides, I wasn't sure where to start. I set the thought aside and ground my teeth for better days.

I've been having those thoughts again.

Portland

We've been here a month. After the endless clogged freeways and sky-piercing cost of living in the Bay Area, I love this place. I remember being excited to leave California. I couldn't afford to buy a house; there were earthquakes; it was crowded. Portland has a cozy charm that reminds me of North Carolina, albeit rainier. Yes, it's self-aware here. Yes, the facial-hair topiary and the whiskey speakeasies do get a bit redundant. The nerds who made money in tech and could afford to upcycle themselves as the Cool Kids have moved here and now sneer at everyone less shellacked and shabby-chic than themselves. The transit system's good but the closest station is kind of a hike.

I like the trains but it's faster to drive. My partner—the aforementioned rebound, let's call him Terry—has just found a job: part-time, retail, at a Body Shop knockoff. Shower gels, lotions, bath scrubs, that kind of thing. It is, of course, my fault that he gave up full-time employment as a receptionist at an upscale Manhattan salon and flew across the country to live with me. He reminds me of this at least daily.

This morning, the ranting turns to a dark aria. Whatever's gotten into him, it started last night: I picked him up from work, drove him home, and the raving commenced: "*I hate this place! I can't make any money! How is it that you work with deaf people and some of them are on benefits, and they have more money than I do! I want to get on disability too! I'm going to go to the top of a tall building, jump off, and break both of my legs. That would be easier than this.*"

Now, in the car, more of same. I don't know what has set him off. It doesn't matter. I pull over. When he sees that I'm crying, he abruptly stops mid-tirade: "*I'm sorry. I'm sorry. I'm sorry.*"

Seattle

We're homeless. Technically. According to the official definition of the term. Although we're not on the street, I planned for that. We came close, too. The ASL interpreter-referral agency I worked for in Portland was lying about its finances, not paying my colleagues and me in full and on time when we invoiced. When you freelance, some fluctuation is part of the deal. But I'd submit an invoice for $1500 and get a third of that if I was lucky. Nobody warned me, either. They were afraid to. The classes I interpreted at the local community college and the occasional jobs I got from another agency were

67

all that kept us fed and kept the lights on. But summer was coming; the Northwest still hadn't recovered from the tech slump; the work would dry up until fall.

"Get a job at Starbucks," my father kept insisting. When I told him my hourly rate as an interpreter was so much higher than what I'd make as a barista that I'd make less in full-time work slinging coffee than scraping by on ten hours a week in my real job, he refused to believe it. This was not a new pattern with him, however. He's hard of hearing. As a kid, I thought his obduracy was about his hearing loss. In adulthood, my experiences with the deaf community taught me a lot about the difference between hearing and listening.

But looking ahead and having no work on my schedule, nor the prospect of much, and my savings depleted from the move up from California, my credit cards maxed, and my regrettably audible partner to support, I could connect the dots. The arc pointed down. I started looking for a storage unit and a place to park the car while we lived out of it.

What saved us: Terry's cousin in Seattle had a spare bedroom in her condo, and offered it to us. A family emergency was metastasizing, so it made sense for us to be closer anyway. Besides, Seattle is Terry's hometown; he moved up here a few weeks ahead of me. The cousin already had a futon set up. It was that or my Honda. With the last of my money, we rented a storage unit, schlepped as much of our stuff up I-5 as we could fit in my Civic, and I've made weekly trips for the last month.

Now when I wake up and get ready for work, I open the door and come face-to-face with last night's adventures. Still neck-deep in her nightlife phase, the cousin likes cocaine and Black men twice her size. It's not unusual in the morning to find some guy crashed out on the sofa and a pile of blow on the coffee table. These visitors rarely come to fully dressed. If I'm honest, I don't mind: I'm not into coke but I applaud her taste in men. She won't struggle back to consciousness for a few more hours. I make coffee, offer this morning's guest a cup. Looking sheepish and a bit the worse for wear, he declines, puts his shirt on, and leaves. I don't catch his name.

Portland

It's my last full day in Portland. Terry's already in Seattle, and I'll be on the road soon enough.

The couple who own the interpreting agency are a pair of thieves. We'll call him James and her Melinda. James, or so the story goes, has pancreatic cancer. He's also gay, and she's a lesbian, but they're married. Or something. It's very confusing and modern. I don't care about that part today. They owe me almost three thousand dollars. I've come to collect it.

When the starving, scared interpreters who work for them ask for the money they're owed, the stock response is, "We can't pay you yet because the client hasn't paid us." No other agency does this. We all know it's a lie. But these two almost monopolize interpreting assignments in Portland. They're not the only game in town but they're the biggest. Piss them off and they'll cut you off, and good luck with that.

To those who press, Excuse Two is deployed: "Oh, it's so terrible. You know James has cancer, right? We're really struggling right now. Can you be patient with us?"

Today, I'm insistent: "My partner's mother up in Seattle is *actually* dying of pancreatic cancer. Since I know you understand what that's like first-hand, you'll understand why I'm going to sit on your sofa until you pay me. After that, I'm getting on I-5 and driving up there. For good. The sooner you write me a check, the sooner I can get on the road."

These are things I know:

James is the apple-cheeked picture of zaftig, besequined good health. Terry's mother is a talking skeleton wrapped in a layer of skin as thin and translucent as a spring-roll wrapper. The end will come for her soon. She misses dancing. James and Melinda bought another company and are hemorrhaging money. Their scheme of not paying Portland's interpreters is all that's propping them up. If James really has cancer, I have green hair, one eye, and three dicks. I'm going to break up with Terry. But I need my own place to live first. Which is why I'm not leaving this place without a check in hand.

Melinda keeps me waiting four and a half hours.

At long last, she flounces into the lobby with the grace of something manufactured by John Deere. "Good news! I checked our books, and the clients have paid us. Not every bit of it, you understand, but enough that you should be happy." She's smiling and her eyes are telling me to go fuck myself. The check is a few hundred dollars short, but it will do. We both know it's rush hour now: by stalling, she's doubled the length of my drive to Seattle. I'll be lucky to get there by ten. I thank her and leave.

Washington, DC

I've just bought the car. It's a '97 Honda Civic sedan, black, quiet, comfortable. First car I've ever bought new. When you buy a new car, you have to drive it carefully for the first few thousand miles. Break the engine in gently. Don't accelerate too hard, don't stomp on the brakes, don't drive like you're at the Nürburgring.

My muscle memory still has muscle memory of finding the Honda's predecessor stolen. From in front of a church in central Baltimore, of all places. A friend from work was getting married. She asked me to be one of the interpreters. For the reception, everyone was meant to drive over to some waterfront restaurant. Except when I went outside after the ceremony, my car wasn't there.

Not possible, I remember thinking before an unsettling belief settled in. *Who'd steal a green manual-transmission Toyota Tercel?*

Someone did.

Now I'm on my way up Wisconsin Avenue to the Maryland suburbs. There's a cluster of federal agencies in Bethesda: Walter Reed, the National Institutes of Health. I have an appointment at the latter: a meeting that should last about an hour. It'll be boring but I like the deaf guy.

For drivers, DC is confusing until you get used to it. The traffic and the buses are the same as you'd find in any large city, and the roads are wide, on a grid, and named alphabetically. Like French grammar, the problem with L'Enfant's urban blueprint is the exceptions: the traffic circles, the tunnels, the parkways that begin in unexpected places and swoop through the city with minimal signage. They're useful but you have to know where they go or else there's no telling where you'll end up.

Just up ahead and to my right, a woman on the sidewalk screams and drops her parcels. She is Asian. Shoulder-length hair. Wearing a purple jacket. Looks like she's just been shopping at Mazza Gallerie or Nieman-Marcus. She's looking at the maroon Ford Taurus sedan that's just come to a stop on a side street. There's something under the Ford. It's light blue. A tarpaulin, I think.

Then it hits me: *It's a woman.* I stomp on the brakes, new-car admonitions be damned. Outside, around me, people are screaming. I realize what's under the Ford at the very same moment its driver does. He tries to reverse. I guess he's in a panic and thinks this will free the person beneath his car. It doesn't work. I'm close enough now to see one of the tires crush the woman's chest when the car backs up.

There's nothing I can do, so in the interest of not blocking traffic, I find the closest parking lot, pull in, and... call my office to let them know I'm going to be late for my assignment.

"What the *fuck* is wrong with me?" I ask this question out loud, disconnect the call before someone answers, and call 911 to report the emergency. I'm not the first, says the voice on the other end of the line. Help is on the way. I then call my office back, tell them what happened, and proceed home too shaken—not just by what I've seen but by my own reaction—to even consider driving up to NIH.

The agency schedules me to interpret a memorial service a few days later. Open casket. Someone kindly asks if I'm afraid of the remains. I'm not. I'm appalled, not afraid. When I get home afterward, I spend the rest of the night researching San Francisco: looking for apartments, interpreting agencies, information about utilities, and so on. Up till now, I've never seriously thought about moving to Northern California, nor even randomly thought about it. Nor have I even been there. The decision comes to me complete, already made, a found object. I'm sure bigger moves to more distant places have been decided upon based on less.

There's an ice dome in the refrigerator. Manufactured around the time Jimmy Carter left office, the fridge creaks when you open the doors. The reek of decades of leftovers pours out: pots of sauce gone sour in the remote back corners, vegetables rotted down to olive-black mush in the crisper, doggie bags and takeout boxes stacked up and wedged in. Frost from the freezer melts and (I guess) trickles down through a crack between the compartments. Hence the dome. It's a terrible stalactite, a big frozen chode. It presses against the top shelf. It's getting bigger. Things are frozen into it: packages of luncheon meat, a container of kimchi. The ice is yellowish grey. I try not to touch it.

I'm past caring how Terry feels about things. His cousin has moved out, rented a place in the city center. She commutes down to Tacoma for work. Better to be closer to the station and the clubs. When the time comes to retrieve our furniture from Portland, Terry melts down on the train. On repeat: *Why do we have to spend hours going down there. Why didn't we rent a U-Haul in Seattle and drive it down instead of taking the train. It's too much trouble. We should just leave it all in the storage unit and buy new stuff.*

"With what?" I ask him.

We're at that stage of a breakup where one partner goes cold and the other one panics. Terry's angry all the time. He's back to square one, looking for a job again, no car, tired of taking the bus, and his mom's dying. Okay, he's allowed to be a disaster. But he is also a mistake I don't need to keep making.

When the end comes, it's horrendous: more for him than for me. His family decides that since I have a job and he doesn't, I should stay in the condo. They all know I've been supporting him. He moves in with his cousin downtown. The landlady—his auntie—has replaced the disgusting refrigerator too. Like the apartment now that I'm finally alone, the new fridge is blessedly clean and silent.

And in that echoing silence, my own ice dome finally cracks. Apart from a couple of friends—the kind you like but aren't close to and will run out of things to talk about with inside of an hour—I don't know anyone else in Seattle. There's a park across the street and a convenience store two blocks away; otherwise, nothing within walking distance. I'm lonelier than I've ever been in my life, yet more relieved as well. I lose so much weight so fast that my trousers fall down in Whole Foods one night, but there's a certain chilly clarity: this doesn't have to be my life. I'm going to get as far away from all this as I can.

Osan, Korea

My American colleague and I are chatting with the head of the English Department. The academic year is wrapping up; our performance reviews have been very good. She is happy with us. Talk turns to holiday plans. The colleague wants to go home to the US; I'm in a long-distance thing with a man in Hong Kong, and we're talking about meeting up in Taipei or Shanghai. Buying plane tickets is troublesome, though.

"Why is that?"

I can't buy them online because I no longer have an American bank account. I did, but on my last trip to Shanghai, someone stole my card details and used it to buy plane tickets, Persian rugs, and all manner of other shit before I finally convinced Washington Mutual to close the account. Between the purchases and the overdraft charges, the damage came to about $9000. I've been reimbursed for most of it, but the bank's policy of referring overdrawn accounts to collections means I've been getting voicemail messages from agents. I delete them without listening. So: my credit is shot, no fault of my own. So: no US card, and our Korean debit cards don't work for online purchases.

"That's... preposterous! Can't you use credit cards?"

"The banks won't issue them to us because we're foreigners."

Professor K. turns several shades of purple, then picks up the phone. I understand Korean well enough to know she's called the campus branch of Korea Exchange Bank. I feel sorry for the person on the other end of the line. This goes on for a few minutes. After the department head hangs up, she tells my colleague and me to stop by the bank tomorrow. It's been sorted out.

I take Daesung, one of my students, a friendly guy who spent years in Canada, along to interpret. The teller asks for both of the cards attached to my account: the ATM card, which is only used for cash withdrawals; and the Visa debit card that should work for online shopping but doesn't. She then hands me two new ones.

"*This* debit card is for ATMs and buying things here in Korea," Daesung explains, pointing to it. "It's like the two old cards put together. And the credit card: it'll work online, and you can use it in other countries."

Having understood some of this, the teller chimes in with a few more details. I wait for Daesung.

"But she wants to remind you that your ATM card—this new one—will not work outside of Korea."

A rime of frost coats the walls. I ask, "*It won't work?* So the old

75

card would let me withdraw money anywhere and the new one won't?"

Daesung looks embarrassed. "It's because you're a foreigner."

"What if I need cash?"

He asks the teller this question, waits for the answer, then interprets it: "Take a lot with you?"

I need a couple of seconds. Then: "How is that safe?"

In the last few months, I've been followed down the street late at night and called a 씨발외국인 (fucking foreigner). An editor I do some work for at the *Korea Herald* has been stabbed. No taxi would take him to the hospital because he was white. I've had to break into my own building because the university put it up for sale and decided I didn't need a key to the front door. Late the same night, I glued the locks open so I wouldn't have to climb up the wall like a burglar again.

In the coming weeks, I will find that this policy has been quietly rolled out across the country. Some banks have stopped issuing cards that will work overseas for new accounts only. Others have cut off that functionality on existing accounts… without first warning the customers. Online, I read horror stories of foreign residents of Korea being stranded abroad, unable to access their own funds. One guy and his family got stuck in Phuket. Another, Vladivostok. And those are just the ones I hear about first.

"Thank you," I say after some consideration. "I think I'm done."

Daesung's face falls. "I understand," he says. "I've left before, too."

Hong Kong

Week after week, the violence cascades into more violence. My husband S. and I have participated in most of the huge marches, but now we're talking about avoiding them. It's getting too dangerous. Besides, I'm a white American. My presence there could be used to feed narratives. Friends closer to the epicenter have suggested I take a step back.

"What has to happen for us to go to the airport?" I ask S. one night over dinner.

On the news, tonight's awfulness is unfolding. One highrise housing estate looks much like the next when it's fogged in with tear gas. I ask what district this is. S. doesn't know either. We've lost track. It's hard to watch but we can't look away. Oh look, they've brought the water cannon out. Oh great, it's the sound cannon that gives you brain damage and makes you shit yourself. I need more wine.

"I don't know," he muses. "They've already killed people. Maybe if they declare a curfew? Put the city under martial law?"

Things get worse. Friends in various states begin offering houses. My sister does too, the difference being that she wants to charge us for it. Our (gay) cousin in Delaware has just bought a big townhouse and sends his address and a message to just text him if we're on our way. *Get out of there*, people keep telling us.

The airport discussion evolves. When the government begins shutting down individual MTR stations, then entire lines, then the whole rail network, we're effectively under a curfew. You can still get around if you drive or take a taxi, but you never know when the roads will be blocked and on fire. Besides, the cops might shoot tear-gas canisters at your windows. Some of the bus lines are running, but that's unpredictable too. Scuffles and clashes flare up all over the city. And two or three places along the tram's route across Hong Kong Island are regular flashpoints. For all intents and purposes,

77

we're trapped in our neighborhood.

We have the cat chipped. He objects, but the vet wins that argument.

"What has to happen for us to grab him and run to the airport?" I ask again when we get home afterward.

We're effectively under martial law. There are black-clad stormtroopers at the entrances to most MTR stations. They grab young people off sidewalks and in shopping malls. Wrong place, wrong time, off to jail or worse.

"I don't know, tanks down Nathan Road?"

Tanks are a sore spot with Hong Kongers. According to local lore, the authorities behind the Tiananmen Square Massacre back in '89 deployed them to crush dead and dying protestors' bodies down to an unidentifiable substance called pie (not the exact word, but that's how it translates, roughly) which could then be scraped off the pavement and disposed of. There were acid baths too, and immolations. Nathan Road is Kowloon's main north-south corridor, and although it isn't a straight shot down from Shenzhen, it's the kind of street an occupying force would use to make a point. We don't get tanks down Nathan Road, but we get other kinds of military transport vehicles. And yet, somehow we stay.

We keep having the same conversation, though: When do we leave? What will it take? When does it finally become too much?

As one violent nightmare week crashes into the next, we keep asking ourselves that. The answer always seems to be just a little worse, just a little worse, just a little bit worse.

Alone again in a crowded room. Or a crowded departure hall, that is. As with many airports designed before the advent of low-cost airlines, Thessaloniki's lacks adequate seating and the layout makes no sense. After security, there's nothing but a grim convenience store, a ransacked deli, and a queue for the washrooms. I wish someone had warned me.

I've been in Greece for a conference. I gave one of the keynotes, in fact. The university's based up in Florina, a town near the border with North Macedonia. It's quiet and hilly; it bakes under the late-summer Mediterranean sun. Olive groves shimmer in the distance. Due to its elevation, it isn't quite as hot as other parts of the country. It reminds me of the San Francisco Bay Area: same topography, similar climate. Florina, I'm told, is the only place in Greece where it snows. Okay, that's one difference. Honestly, there's not much on offer—you can see the whole place in a day and no tourists visit—but the food's delicious and the people are great. When they learn where I live, the reaction is consistent: concerned, erudite horror.

Even here, Hong Kong is big news, but no one knows the extent of it. The protests at the airport shocked the world. I wasn't sure I'd be able to get out of there. Now I'm not sure I'll be able to get back. If it comes to that, I have a multiple-entry visa for China and can fly into Guangzhou or Shenzhen and make my way home by train. The trains will keep running even if the airport shuts down. I think. My Mandarin's not great, but I'll manage. There have been some 1300 arrests so far. Cops forcing prisoners to burn their own eyeballs with laser pointers. Beating prisoners they've already subdued. Stomping on their hands to break the bones. Dragging bleeding patients out of hospitals to arrest them. Shooting tear gas and pepper balls at journalists. And, more recently, a couple of weeks before this trip, attacking passengers in an MTR station and on the train and going on such a rampage that several are rumored to have been killed. The question is less about whether I can get back than it is about what conditions will be like when I finally do.

Most of the conference attendees teach at universities. Some are grad students. They all understand the hitch in my throat when I talk about my students who have gone missing. I've become friends with one of the conference delegates from Thessaloniki. She was kind enough to drop me off at the airport on her way home. In the car, somewhere in the middle of northern Greece, I check Twitter for news from Hong Kong. Two 13-year-olds have just been arrested during one of the protests. I can't tell if they were participants or simply in the wrong place at the wrong time. Knowing what has been happening to people who get arrested there, I come unglued, crying in the car of this woman I just met.

This terrible waiting area contains about three times as many passengers as it was designed for. Lacking seats, people perch on their suitcases or just sit on the floor. I don't want dust on my ass, so I pace, watching the departure board for updates, praying my flight to Istanbul won't be delayed, praying that it will.

Seattle

What saved me: Several friends knew what was happening. One of them paid off the loan on my car. Two others sent funds to keep me (us) fed until my first paycheck from the new agency arrived. No point in asking my family for help. They won't. I've tried. They treat me like I'm still the high school student who got in trouble back in the day, an endless and largely undiscussed narrative of punishment and contempt, and seem to wonder why I live on the other side of the country and have mostly stopped talking to them.

"I'm literally homeless."

It's your own fault. Get a job at Starbucks.

"I'm living with a guy who loses his shit and screams at me."

It's your own fault. Gay men are like moths that fly into candle flames.

I'm bored, burnt out, and in constant grinding pain from repetitive strain injuries. Nothing about my life then or now is sustainable. Now that I'm in Seattle, drowning in rainfall and silence, there's enough time to think and little else to do. Years ago, a high school friend chucked everything and moved to Japan to teach English. Made some money there. Met his wife. I do some research. Seems it's really a thing. Best of all, you can live below your means. In the online forums I stay up until 3am reading night after night, people talk about how much they save each month, how much they've got in the bank. You can do pretty well in Japan, even better in Korea. Your employer pays your airfare and your rent. The cost of living is cheap. It will give me time. Freelancing is an endless scramble for work, and there's never a sense that my time is actually free. Agency positions aren't much better. In Asia, I'll have travel opportunities I wouldn't otherwise get. Professional ones too, I expect. And with the money I imagine I'll save, I can finally think about grad school. It'll be a big move to a distant place, but there's justification and I'm great at departures. Besides, it couldn't possibly be worse than what I'm leaving behind. Probably much safer, too.

Cornwall

It would be vulgar to contemplate faking one's death with a pandemic raging. I no longer do. For two years now, we have lived with this. Lived *through* this. First in Hong Kong (I think I had Covid before the public knew what it was), then here. Two years of grim terror and lockdowns. A second layer of terror waiting for my work visa to be approved. Everything about this past year in Cornwall has been a reflection of my time in Seattle. Throbbing, viral silence. Throat-shredding sobs with no one to hear them. Waking up in a panic at 3am feeling as if the blankets are strangling me like the tentacles of a kraken, dragging me down into depths from which I'll never resurface. Sit up gasping, startle the cat. Drink some water from the bottle I keep by the bed. Do I put on some clothes and go out for a walk, just for fresh breaths of clean air? It's pouring outside but so what? There will be oxygen. Or do I just get up and go to the bathroom, then come back to bed and hope for the best? Perhaps I'm already dead. It would explain a lot.

There's a departures committee observing my comings and goings, counting down until it's time to drive me forth into the world again. Britain ought to be scared or relieved. I've lived in more places than most people, and left every one. Or escaped, really. After multiple rounds of that, I don't know what it's like to be present. But with Covid surging and England drunk-walking in and out of lockdowns, there are lessons if I'm willing to receive them. This is my life now. This is going to be my life for some time to come, and I think I'm okay with that, inasmuch as I have any say in the matter. I'd prefer to remain. Now to figure out how.

THE FIBONACCI
GRAWLIX (OR:
BULLSHIT REPELLANT)

1.

Soap tastes bitter. Like many Generation X kids in the South, you have your mouth washed out a few times for cussing. The floral, slippery nastiness rasps against your tongue and the insides of your cheeks; the astringency puckers your tongue like sweet vinegar, and the suds scud around your mouth, multiplying in your spit. Some instinct tells you they're toxic. You try not to swallow, but inevitably you do, just a little, and gag. The textures in your throat go all wrong. There's more gagging. It's not a thing you forget. Like many dour Silent Generation parents, yours believe in *Do as we say, not as we do.* You can be very literal, though. And kids learn language by parroting their parents. Ex-Marine veterans with PTSD cuss in the same way the sun comes up in the east, axiomatically. What ensues is inevitable. You don't like being a kid. *Damn* and *shit* hold a power you want. If you could scroll the clock forward, you would. *Those words don't sound good in kids' mouths*, you were told. You wanted to reply *Then stop giving us reasons to say them.* You didn't, though. You don't.

In your South, backtalk is much worse than cussing. Soap would be dessert in comparison. You keep your mouth shut. You swallow the words you want to say. They taste like soap going down.

2.

When your parents don't socialize and then suddenly they do, your paradigms burst like ripe pomegranates. Quiet after-school afternoons of reruns give way to swim practice at six and then dinner. Sitcoms. The evening news. You're not sure how adult conversations work. The adults you know talk *at*, not *with*: you, each other, everyone. There are outbursts of yelling or screaming, but mostly there is extended silent awkwardness. Because of the Cold War, you all know you could die any minute. With all its military targets, eastern North Carolina would be cratered in the first wave. There is therefore a backdrop of tension and swearing. So when your parents go to a party—they've never done *that* before!—and come home with a gag gift, you're a bit lost. It's a spray can from Spencer's, a place you will later learn also sells naughty flotsam like lava lamps, edible panties, and motion lotion—lube that heats up when you have sex. The can's label reads Bullshit Repellant. Someone has helpfully put a thin strip of tape over the brown word. It covers the bottom half of the letters. Try as you might, you can't tell what it's for, what it does, how it helps. You have no words for this.

3.

You aren't supposed to say *shit* but *BS* is sort of okay, an allowable workaround, or so you thought. At age six, you haven't heard the phrase *grey area* yet but would have recognized the idea behind it. No fan of grey, your teacher has black-and-white views on what kind of language her students should use. Since someone helpfully put tape over the **Bullshit Repellant**'s offensive syllable, you figured it would be okay to bring it to class for Show and Tell. "See, it's BS Repellant!" you exclaim, and get sent to the office. The principal is known to have a big wooden paddle with holes drilled into it. According to friends who've been spanked with it, the modified paddle will swing through the air faster and hit your backside harder than a normal one, forcing little half-domes of stinging buttmeat up and into the holes. The pain is a legend, an epic. The principal glares at you across her immense desk. "What does BS stand for? Do you know what the letters mean?" Of course you do. "Do you know what it means? If you do, prove it by saying the words." You burst into tears. The paddle hangs on the wall behind her left shoulder. If she wants, she could turn around and pluck it off its hook without getting out of her chair. "Bull... *shoot?*" you mumble between sobs. "You know that's not it," she says. "Say the words." You aren't bawling because you're afraid, exactly, or remorseful. But she keeps insisting that you say the word *bullshit* because she *wants* to hit you; she's getting mad because she wants the excuse and you refuse to give it to her. You keep on sobbing and she sends you back to class. This is a personal first: you didn't allow yourself to be beaten.

4.

If *shit* is the dirtiest word for obvious reasons and *hell* the most dangerous because you've seen *The Exorcist* and know what could go wrong, that relegates *damn* to a sort of PG status: hardly nice but not the worst. One day a friend—we'll call him Todd—asks if you want to know the filthiest cussword of them all. If you say it and your parents find out, you'll be in trouble for the rest of your life. Of course you want to know. He leads you outside, through the back yard, and out onto the golf course behind your house. There, standing on the little bridge that separates two water traps, Todd looks around to make sure no one else is in earshot. He then says the word *fuck*, and spells it: F-U-C-K. You don't believe him at first. It sounds contrived, artificial, a bit stupid. You were expecting a spell or a ceremony or at least more syllables, not this ugly little cough of a word. Is this a prank? Had he made it up? You begin to doubt your doubts. It does have four letters. And it means *sexual intercourse*, that mysterious grownup activity kids your age know involves beds and genitals and possibly a stork. You ask, "Are you sure it's real?" When he nods, you take your new favorite word for a spin: "Fuck fuck fuck fuck fuck fucking fuck. Fuck fuck fuck." The look of panic on Todd's face is the sweetest reward you could have imagined.

5.

Joining a swim team in your early teens guarantees awkwardness.

You're a thin Lycra strip short of naked at a time in your life when you least want to be. Things are growing: legs, parts, bits. The changes are visible, clearly outlined, hard to miss. Boundaries fray. Locker-room talk coalesces. The boys, whose voices are deeper now, mainly rhapsodize about the girls' sudden breasts. How they'd love to put their faces between them and make motorboat noises. There are tall tales about climbing up on top of the lockers, lifting one of the drop-ceiling tiles out of its frame, and crawling through the gym's ribcage in order to peep down into the girls' locker room. All those titties and butts, maybe glimpses of pussy. Of course none of it's real, but the boys talk about it. *Perform* talking about it. They brag. You stay quiet but try to project the same air of naughty, proto-masculine merriment. You're friends with the girl whose boobs were the first to develop, and by far the biggest. It's how you learned the word *pontoons*. One evening at practice, she takes you aside and whispers "Look *at that.*" You follow her gaze. The nerdy, skinny boy nobody talks to or likes much has somehow sprouted a grown man's cock. It bulges like a sock in the front of his Speedo, so much so as to be a little mortifying. You don't admit it, but you've already noticed. So has everyone else. No one talks about that, not even in the locker room. There are glances. Subtle tensions. Everything is plainly visible, but everything is covered up. We prefer to pretend it's not there. We need to be protected from it.

6.

You yourself *are* the unsayable. You're aware of this. There's a grawlix—that camouflage of ampersands, asterisks, and exclamation marks that hides vowels and makes bad words more acceptable— over your identity. Everybody can see it. At school you're called a f@g and a q^**r more times a day than you can count, and you're good at math. Everybody can see that too. So you yourself are this unspeakable thing, but the word itself is allowed when directed at you. You're obsessed with this paradox. It teaches you things. These words exist to annihilate, to ostracize. The message: *You're worse than sh!t because you want to get f^cked up the @ss, and you're probably going to h&ll, you disgusting q^**r.* No one puts a stop to it. No one gets in trouble. Unlike the other varieties, this type of swearing is somehow permitted; encouraged, even.

7.

You use up all the **Bullshit Repellant** trying to work out what the stuff smells like. The opposite of actual literal shit, perhaps: metal-lic and slightly industrial. Half disinfectant spray, half WD-40. You spray a puff in the air in front of a window and watch the drop-lets settle like little similes on every surface, then another puff, then another, until the can is empty. You could use some today. Grawl-ixes spread exponentially, or logarithmically. Presidents cuss now; platforms have proliferated; and yet, for all this dirty talk, there's so much less we can say. You've spent your whole life in open rebellion against a mouthful of hand soap—being told what not to say, what not to be. Today's backtalk is a tide of clapback. You won't get your mouth washed out for using strong language, nobody will; at most, there might be a few symbols over your words, little glyphs that hark back to the days when typebars struck sheets of clean paper.

8.

The camouflage remains for as long as it can. You already know what the lumps and the bulges are, what they look like. The shapes are quite clear. They get bigger as the years pass. Eventually you have to uncover all the letters, to read and be read. As a young adult, when you embraced your status as the unsayable, your vocabulary changed. You found delicious new layers of nuance in the chatty sordidness of gay conversation behind closed doors: the smidge of emphasis on the first syllable of *cocktail*, the linguistic versatility of *shit*, the useful directionality of *fuck*. Nothing is covered up. This language is a compass, and that's just the start. Many of the older guys you meet lace their sentences with articulate filth. It's a revelation. It's oddly charming. Also, you *understand*. Every thunderswear that follows some minor mishap like running out of gin or spilling tea on your lap points to the story you share: They didn't like being kids either. The words still have power. They taste amazing in the mouths of grown men.

TARDINESS: A
PERSONAL HISTORY

Truro, England: June 2021

I'm in trouble.

After almost a year here, I've committed the drive down to Falmouth into muscle memory. I know the curves in the road, the lanes I'll need at the roundabouts, the lights I'll most likely catch red. Most of the time, the commute takes just under an hour door to door. There's the eastward leg through suburbia toward central Truro: a couple of retail parks I rather like, a long row of identical semi-detached   houses I can't imagine buying or renting because who wants to live on a clogged thoroughfare?, a speed camera or two. There's the hill as you descend from Gloweth and Highertown into the city center (which isn't called Lowertown but ought to be). You pass a big pub called the County Arms shortly before you reach the congested roundabout where the parking lots for Aldi, Sainsbury's, and the Cornwall County Hall all converge. The office parks I drive past could be anywhere—I've seen similar in places as far apart as Charlotte and Chiang Mai, Stockholm and Sydney—but in this drizzly tidiness of cute houses with gardens that dazzle with late-spring flowers, you couldn't be anywhere other than this southwest-ernmost corner of England. It's easy to be overwhelmed by the lush greenery. It rains like you're on Venus but the atmosphere won't kill you, and there's always the threat of lapsing into Stendhal syndrome because of the rampant gorgeousness of it all.

When the fall semester began, I was still not used to driving in Britain and, doubly paranoid, would give myself an hour and a half to get to work. I'd just moved to the UK from Hong Kong and my PTSD had PTSD. You can only inhale so much teargas and run from unhinged paramilitaries masquerading as cops so many times before your blood turns into pure cortisol. No one leaving that city in the wake of 2019 will emerge unscathed. As time passed and I grew less terrified that my mind would wander and a head-on collision would ensue (I'm American), I learned how much time I would need. I didn't mind cutting it close. Because of the pandemic, I wasn't keen to spend more time on campus and around other people than necessary. My approach: get there, teach the class, speak from a safe distance of six feet away to any students I needed to chat with afterward, race back home at five miles an hour below the speed limit, lock the door. Now and then traffic could be a bit slow. Rain and rush hour even during lockdown could take their toll. And time and space got melty during England's endless, shifting lockdowns. Could we go to the shops this week or not? What was open, what was closed? Where could you go, exactly? No one seemed to know, and Britain's elected officials flagrantly did whatever they wanted to anyway, regardless of what this week's rules were. I never felt entirely certain of anything. No one did.

This morning, I gave myself what I thought was enough of a buffer. Even a last-minute trip to the loo hasn't thrown me off schedule by much. I've had IBS all my life. Making provisions for that third or fourth trip to the bathroom has always been a part of the morning routine. I checked traffic before I left. Nothing too unusual, maybe a little slow on the A390 until the roundabout at the hospital entrance and the retail park. Two lanes of traffic converge just after you pass it. I was certain I'd have enough time but traffic's not moving. This modest little city of 30,000 anchors a wider region of ten times that. But when the tourists come, nothing moves. I don't think I'll make it to campus on time, and I'm supposed to be teaching a workshop on creative writing to a group of teachers visiting from other parts of the country. At this rate, it'll take me half an hour just to get to the Arch Hill roundabout, where I'll turn right to take the A39 down to Falmouth. That'll leave me another half-hour to drive the entire way, find parking, and hike up the hill to my office. Not impossible, but the best-case scenario is that I'll arrive late and panting. Not the best first impression. I'm so screwed.

Greenville, NC: 1982

Here's what it's like to be the class fag pariah in the small-town American South. Every school had a few kids like this. Back in the day, you just took the abuse and the taunting. No one would help because the consensus held that it was your own fault for being that way in the first place. I used to sit on the long bench in the atrium either reading or writing. One day, a couple of boys came up and took a seat on either side of me, boxing me in. One said, "Well, I'll be a monkey's uncle! Does yours look like that?" as he slid a picture of a naked man cut out of a porno mag onto the pages of my book. The cock was huge, red, and fully erect. Too shocked to say anything, I tried to push the slip of paper away. "Mine looks like that," the boy continued. "Does that turn you on? Do you wish you could

92

suck it?" Was he talking about his own dick or the porn model's? Did he even catch the ambiguity? I spluttered, got up, and hurried to the guidance counselor's office to hide. There were no windows but there were also no students, just an unoccupied sofa and no one who would hit me or shove gay porn in my face. I was twelve.

Coping strategy: I began to time everything to avoid everybody. Between classes, I'd linger at my locker, sometimes reading but also scanning for oncoming thugs. Although I didn't get beaten up much (at school, anyway), the taunting was relentless. So by keeping my distance and killing time, I could then race into class at the last minute, thereby saving myself from the few minutes of hissed questions I'd otherwise get: "Where's your *boyfriend*, Marshall?" "Did you run funny like that because you just took it up the ass?" "What does sperm taste like?"

There was always a balance to this. Being one of those bright kids who got straight As with no effort, I couldn't afford to get in trouble for being late. I could get away with it to a certain extent, but I had to be careful. If I was going to have an escape hatch other than a noose or a bottle of my mother's pills, it would have to be my report cards. My teachers knew what was going on but, well, it was the South and, you know, Reagan. Faggots got laughed at back then, at least until they started dying *en masse*, and then they still got laughed at.

Harm reduction: some 15 years before I heard the term for the first time, I was already practicing it by darting into the classroom just as the bell rang, or two seconds after.

Truro, England: June 2021

The Arch Hill roundabout scares me a little. If you look at a map of Truro, you'll see that the A390 curves south around the city center. My husband S. once said it looks like a man's crotch in underwear. He has a point. At the southernmost point in the bulge, Arch Hill (aka the A39) takes you south toward Falmouth. Despite and because of the amount of traffic flowing through here, there are no lights at this intersection, just two interlocking roundabouts that maim visitors. There *should* be lights, but Truro's too small to have an alternate route to use while the works are being carried out. In the quieter seasons, the system sort of works if everyone knows how to use it. But when it's raining, visibility is poor, and there are tourists, accidents happen.

My heart always speeds up as I approach it. I've had two near misses. The first time, turning right one early morning, I was distracted and anxious. Did I have the right of way? Did the other car? Probably they did, but I realized this when I was already in the roundabout. I floored the gas pedal. Thank god for good pickup. Almost crapped myself. Got to campus still shaking. The second time, I almost hit a police car that was turning right onto the A390 from Old Falmouth Road. I had literally not realized that a route through the twin roundabouts existed. Plus, it was raining. I stomped the brakes. The cop in the passenger's seat turned to glare at me, rapping his knuckles on the car window. *Be careful,* he mouthed. On the way home, I stopped in at Sainsbury's not because I needed groceries but because I was terrified they might change their minds and pull me over. Since then, I've grown more comfortable behind the wheel: I've lived here long enough to know who has the right of way, long enough even to swear at obvious tourists as they blunder through these junctions.

Once I'm through the roundabout, I stomp on the gas. There's less traffic now. Speed limits are higher than they would be on similar roads in the States. Southbound Arch Hill curves downward and away from Truro's nutsack. I take comfort in acceleration. The transition from very small city to verdant countryside is instant: stone hedgerows and curtain-walls of trees line the road. It's twisty—no wide, straight American-style thoroughfares here—and there's barely a building in sight. My relief disappears the second I round the first curve and see brake lights. Just ahead, there's an oversized truck creeping forward, no doubt scraping the square-cut tree canopy overhead.

Mercifully, the truck turns at one of the side roads that lead off into the lanes, which is what Cornwall's narrow rural roadways are called. They're also called rat runs. Barely the width of a regular passenger car, most of these are fenced on both sides by hedgerows or ancient stone walls. Sometimes both. They'd be impossible to widen without dynamite, and so much would be required that Cornwall itself would break off and float out into the Atlantic. Brambles scratch your paintwork. Not all of these rat runs are even paved. When two cars meet coming in opposite directions, one person has to back up. Here and there, you'll find driveways or turnouts for passing. Now and then, the local news sites print pictures of cars and trucks wedged between these stone walls—no doubt driven by tourists or emmets (the derogatory local term for newcomers). I'm less terrified of the lanes than I was at first, but locals speed on them. I've faced oncoming death at 60 miles per hour several times, and once a massive lorry came barreling toward me when I rounded a blind corner. It's as frightening as it sounds.

I mark my trek down to work with the roundabouts, and now

I'm at the next one, Playing Place, the real actual name of the first village past Truro. Named for a traditional Cornish open-air theater in the round (in Cornish, it's *Plen an Gwari*), Playing Place is a little suburb of the little city. Like so much else here, it sits on centuries of history and is relevant because there's a Texaco station. I consider pulling off the road, onto the forecourt. Should I text my colleagues? Can someone get a message to someone? But this has all happened at the last minute, and I'm not sure who's doing what or even who I'm meant to be teaching, really. I've got some notes in my iPad and ideas for an activity if I need one. Mostly I'll be ad-libbing this. Freeballing, as it were. As long as traffic doesn't grind to a halt again, I'll be… only slightly late?

Greensboro, NC: 1994

My second job after university was at a small social-services agency for deaf and hard-of-hearing people. This agency is still around, but the name has changed since my time there. There were three full-time staff positions: the director, the office manager, and me. I've forgotten what my job title was—"Interpreter/Consultant," I think. Being the only one of the three even remotely fluent in American Sign Language, I stayed busy. The director's duties seemed to comprise two tasks: long lunches and long intervals of crying in her office. It was her first job out of grad school. She was over her head and out of her depth. The office manager answered the phones and scheduled appointments for interpreters in the Greensboro area when requests came in. I handled day-to-day interpreting needs and a lot of *ad hoc* consultancy services on the newly enacted Americans with Disabilities Act. This entailed endless phone calls to doctors and law firms and such, informing them that they now had to pay for interpreting services instead of us. These calls were not received with much warmth.

The office manager—we'll call her Sharon—couldn't stand me. It was subtle at first, the jeering way she'd comment on the fact that I had a tattoo on "that skinny leg" the first time she saw me in shorts, the way I'd catch her looking at me as if I smelled bad. She often got to work late because she had to drop her daughters off at school. Ergo, if the center was going to open on time, it was imperative that I be there. As time went by, I saw the pattern. She was one of those good Christian ladies who love gay men as long as they're hairstylists. Skinny awkward nerds in social services didn't fit her "love the sinner, hate the sin" religious paradigms, so the power of Christ compelled her to drive me out.

The director—we'll call her Rachel—didn't like me much either. She did at first. But she and Sharon started having closed-door meetings shortly after I got hired. The tone shifted. I was late too often, Rachel said. So was she. She'd rock in at ten or ten-thirty, pale and puffy and in retrospect probably hung over. Her office door would close. She'd emerge for coffee. Little else seemed to get done.

It was a very grey year. We didn't have the Internet, but we'd heard of it. I had no social life to speak of. I didn't drink much. Couldn't afford cable TV. At night I'd get home and read book after book, sometimes more than once if I liked them enough. Time worked differently then. I'd get to the end of the month and sigh with relief that I could finally afford to go to the supermarket. Even though my pay wouldn't be deposited until the last day of every month, checks were a thing then: I could write one a day in advance, knowing it wouldn't bounce. Also, around the 20th of every month, I'd be reimbursed for expenses. It was never much, maybe $50, but it meant I could eat, put gas in the car, and gasp my way through that last week and a half until payday.

I couldn't seem to save money. Nor could I find a part-time job. I did apply for them. No one would hire me. Skinny socially awkward gay nerds were not of interest to the retail sector. Perhaps we are now, but we weren't then. Exhausted from month after month of scraping by, I made an appointment with a financial advisor at a county agency. He reviewed my paltry financials and said, "This is easy. You can't save money because you're literally not making enough to save. You're not wasting it on anything that I can tell. It's not your fault. You're going to have to find another job."

By this point, I had worked out a system: I knew when each bill was due and what the grace period was, and I'd mail out the checks at the last minute so that there would be money in the bank as long as possible for contingencies. Inevitably, some were late. But my credit was already a smoldering Nagasaki to begin with, so I couldn't worry too much about making it worse.

Toward the end of my year at that agency, work I'd done began disappearing off the computers. Notably, one three-day assignment that I'd already given to one of the local interpreters just vanished. The deaf client got upset because they were expecting an interpreter to show up. The hearing client had no idea what was going on. The interpreter lost several hundred dollars as a result. Everyone was inconvenienced and annoyed. Naturally, I got blamed for it. When I suggested that Sharon must have deleted it, she lunged across her desk at me shouting. I asked around. Colleagues in the interpreting community and several local deaf folks knew how she felt about me. The consensus was that she was sabotaging my work. Rachel was too clueless to see it, either hiding in her office in tears or having long lunches with Sharon.

One night I stopped by the supermarket for a big can of the decaf version of the coffee we drank in the office. I'd recently gone off caffeine, a terrible mistake I hope never to repeat, but my two enemies still partook. (I drank a lot of chamomile tea, and Sharon once remarked that it looked like I was drinking urine.) I then drove over to our building, let myself in, and replaced the coffee with decaf. The ensuing withdrawal headaches turned Rachel and Sharon into a pair of bickering monsters. And when Rachel tried to fire me a few weeks later, we had a lovely, enlightening chat about how the center literally could not function without someone fluent in ASL. How would that look in the deaf community? I'd be out there freelancing and getting by, talking with everyone about what had happened, how they'd treated me. Did she *really* think that would be a good idea? She backed down. I found a job in DC. Packed and left. Big relief.

Lesson learned: it's okay if the weepy, hungover director and the straight lady with two kids are always late for work. But if you're gay, you're forever support staff. We'll still despise you, but as long as you show up on time, don't ask questions, and do as you're told, we'll pretend that we're tolerating you. To your face, anyway.

Truro/Penryn, England: June 2021

The next couple of roundabouts come in quick succession: Carnon Downs (no distinguishing features apart from the sign for a chain hotel that's not visible from the road), Bissoe (there's another steep slope and a stretch of dual carriageway where you can finally pass

any trucks you've been stuck behind). Things get a bit more interesting at Treluswell (it rhymes with "it *does* well"). Madame Satellite,
as I've nicknamed the stern voice of my satnav system, always insists
that I turn left. This route would take me through downtown Penryn and to the opposite side of Falmouth. It's not that you can't drive
down both high streets, but why would you? It would take at least
ten minutes longer, and there are electronic bollards in Falmouth. I
don't know how they work. Better to stay on the A390, which takes
you *around* Penryn. From there, it's a straight shot into Falmouth
and down to the waterfront, just a bit beyond campus. If I park in
one of the paid lots, I can avoid the twin terrors of narrow streets
and parallel parking. Besides, I no longer bother with satnav on the
drive to work. Muscle memory and whatnot. But in my first couple
of months here, I had to listen to Madame Satellite bark *"recalculating... recalculating..."* as if she were irked at me for disobeying every
time I passed this way.

"Dogging" is British slang for having sex outdoors. It can take
place almost anywhere, it would seem: parks, parking lots, public toilets. Well, I'm less certain about the latter: I think "cottaging" covers
that one, at least among gay men on the prowl. A local news site published a listicle not long after I got here: popular spots for dogging
in and around Truro. Apparently there's a lot of it going on, straight
people shagging in cars and the woods and on park benches, every
bit as brazen as the gay guys. Raunchy bastards.

In Asia, this isn't a thing. There are love hotels. Although the idea
sounds sleazy *prima facie*, it makes sense there. People live with their
families until well into adulthood. The cities are crowded. If you're
gay, there are saunas and sex clubs, but most couples don't have other
places to fuck. It's all very discreet: frosted glass if there's a lobby,

landscaping and barriers to hide license plates on cars, even vending machines that dispense your room keys. The love-hotel rooms I've seen (strictly for research purposes, of course) are very clean. Your partner might give you scabies but the sheets won't. Sex etiquette in the countries I'm familiar with involves taking a shower first, and after. Considering the weather, it would be disgusting not to.

The lay-by just after Treluswell is a notorious gay cruising spot. Which seems odd. By day, there's a food truck. It does a lot of business. There are a few picnic tables in the adjacent green space. Even in the rain, there are plenty of cars parked out there whenever I pass by... at least, during the day. In the evening, the picture changes. You can only see the entrance and exit to the lay-by from the road. Now and then I've glanced in that direction. From what I could tell, you'd need good parallel-parking skills if you wanted to pop in for quick head in the shrubbery. But I'm baffled just now. How many of these customers are there for a blowjob as well as a breakfast burrito? Day and night, the place does a lot of business. But how does it *work*, exactly? And wouldn't they want to make sure the utensils are clean before putting someone else's fork in their mouth?

It's 11.40am. Again, I'm tempted to pull over and text my colleagues, and pruriently curious about what I might see, but I press on. As long as nothing ghastly happens, I might almost be sort of on-time-ish.

San Francisco, CA: 2003

Ten and I'm in. I used to repeat this phrase in my head, sometimes mouthing the words to reassure myself that I wouldn't be late, I wouldn't be late, I wouldn't be late... knowing it was a lie, of course, and not a spell or incantation. After four years in the San Francisco Bay Area, I had a sense of how the community felt about me: decent interpreter, used to work at Gallaudet University so had an additional bit of professional cred, prone to being late.

I never told people how often I had to detour on my way to work to find a clean restroom in a hurry. I always seemed to be ducking into hotel lobbies, City Hall, Moscone Center, the Metropolitan Community Church on Eureka Street, Stonestown Galleria, you name it. One time I had a job down in San Jose—on campus at San Jose State—and to this day I remember the sweaty terror. When the urge hits, it's a lightning strike. I don't have much time. That morning, I parked. Panicked. The gym was the closest building I thought might be open. The woman at the front door saw my distress and let me in even though I didn't have a campus ID. I made it to the men's room with seconds to spare.

Over the years, I tried and tried to tighten up my habits. I'd leave earlier. Prepare better in advance. Get lunch ready. Make sure my clothes were set out and ironed. In fact, I'd do all the ironing on Sunday afternoons. A whole closet full of wrinkle-free shirts and trousers! All of this helped and none of it mattered: my guts had the last word. Eventually my habit of paying bills at the last possible moment merged with my need to stay at home until the last possible moment. This echoed with earlier time-management choices. Corrosive anxiety is sometimes better than actual risk.

Meanwhile, much of the travel writing I was reading back then put a different spin on punctuality-obsessed (or just work-obsessed) American lifestyles. In *Under the Tuscan Sun*, Frances Mayes famously bailed on the Bay Area after a messy divorce, ended up in Italy, and bought and refurbished a house there. It's a seductive story.

She is gracious in her frustration at how long it takes for her con-
tractors to show up and finish their work. Time is softer there, more
flexible. Tomorrow. Later. Eventually. It'll get done. Tony Cohan re-
counts a similar tale in *On Mexican Time*. Like Mayes, he abandoned
the US for a warmer and more inviting locale south of the border.
Like Mayes, he and his wife fall in love with a charming town (San
Miguel de Allende) and hire men who take forever to refurbish the
house they buy. The more I read in this genre (*A Year in Provence*,
In Maremma, and so on), the more convinced I became that I was
physically not cut out for life in America. Or at a minimum, I was
not cut out for a profession that required me to race all over the
metro area from one assignment to the next, catching the occasional
nap in my car in a parking garage, never knowing quite when traffic
on the freeway would grind to a halt or the streetcar wouldn't come,
always stressed out and gobbling Pepto Bismol tablets, always on the
verge of being late.

Penryn, England: June 2021

Ten and I'm in. This phrase is back in my head again. No, I won't be
in my office in ten minutes, but with only three stoplights between
me and campus, the odds are improving. I've passed the one next to
the campus Falmouth and Exeter share. I stayed in one of the student residences for a couple of months last summer right after I arrived in the UK, while I was looking for a house. The rental market
here in Cornwall is even worse than San Francisco at the height of
the dotcom madness twenty-odd years ago. Dozens of people apply
for every flat and house that goes on the market. Too many AirBnB
properties, too many second homes, too many people down here

from London and Birmingham and Bristol now that they can work remotely. I don't *love* my modest little terrace house in the burbs—it feels like a way station until my husband gets here from Hong Kong and we can buy a place of our own—but I'm grateful to have it nonetheless.

My grandmother used to say she'd get to something "directly," meaning "later, at some unspecified time of my choosing, perhaps not as soon as you'd like even though I'm using a word that suggests immediacy because it will shut you up and because there are other things I might consider more important but would prefer to discuss with you right now." It was, and remains, a useful word, and it's still used down here in Cornwall. We're not of Cornish origin that I know of, but a branch of the family originated just up the A30 in Devon. Perhaps "directly" is part of the family story I've never been told. I find myself saying it more often now that I live here. Like a stonemason or a bricklayer in a sunnier country, I will get to things when I get to them, later and at a time of my choosing.

I've passed the big Asda supermarket now, made a mental note to stop in on the way home. Their dishwasher pods dissolve better than the Sainsbury's ones. There are a few other things I need too, but mainly it's for the dishwasher pods. After Asda, there's a couple-of-mile stretch where although a sign warns of a speed camera, there isn't one. You can speed. So I do. Last roundabout before Falmouth, hang a left, down the steep hill, and the mouth of the River Fal comes into sudden view. It always seems to be low tide, but a broad expanse of sparkling water is never an unwelcome sight, even if you are looking at it from above the rooftops of a couple of chain stores.

It's now 11.50. It'll take me a whisker less than ten minutes to get to campus and park. Instead of going back to my office, I'll go straight to the meeting room where I'm meant to be teaching this workshop. That was my technique back in Hong Kong: I'd have my lesson plans in Google Drive and a couple of whiteboard markers in my backpack. Water bottle already full. Everyone here knows traffic's unpredictable with lockdown over and the tourists back.

I'll be there *directly*.

Hong Kong: 2019

After almost 15 years in hardworking, punctuality-obsessed Asia—first Korea, then Hong Kong—I settled into a sort of compromise state. Some instructors are diligent about being in class and ready to go as soon as the minute hand hits the 12 or the 6. My own students quickly realize I'm the other type, the one who will rock in three minutes late and switch on the classroom PC. I don't make much small talk because I'm an introvert and there's a switch I have to flip in my head first. We'll get started eventually. I ease into things.

My husband and I lived on Caine Road in the lower Mid-Levels my final year there. To get to my university campus out in the remote New Territories, I had to make my way down the hill either on foot (rarely pleasant in that swelter) or in a taxi or minibus. From there, I'd take the MTR out to Kam Sheung Road in far-suburban Yuen Long. Kam Sheung Road isn't a busy station, and it's easy to get a cab there. Although there's a station a short walk from campus, one stop away from the end of that line, there were two issues above and beyond my time-management failings: heat and safety. For much of the year, Hong Kong is hotter than Satan's taint, and the campus is at the top of a gentle rise. Walking, you don't really notice until the final stretch up to the main entrance. There's no shade. The only thing I hate more than getting sweaty in the first place is then having to interact with other people while dripping. Plus, the protests had been going on for months and getting more violent. Skipping Yuen Long Station, where gangland thugs raided an MTR train and beat the shit out of innocent commuters and were largely not prosecuted for it, felt like the smarter thing to do. I still had to pass through there on the way home but if it had been easier to catch a taxi on campus, I'd have preferred that.

It's hard to say where the dividing line was in the protests, the point at which I went from being concerned to being just plain scared all the time. One afternoon in early fall, late September or thereabouts, S. and I walked down the hill to have ramen at a little izakaya we knew to be supportive of the pro-democracy movement. That's a thing there: there are lists of pro-democracy shops and restaurants, places whose owners have made public statements in favor of the cause. This is called the yellow economic circle, in contrast with the pro-Beijing establishment, who are blue. As much as I liked the yellow izakaya, the food didn't seem to like me. We'd eaten there together maybe twice? Each time resulted in rapid-onset digestive Krakatoa. Hiking up a steep hill in stifling heat with literally every muscle in your body clenched to keep the lava inside the volcano is not an experience I would recommend to anyone other than high-level Hong Kong government officials. Perhaps this time, something would be different.

We were planning to go over to Causeway Bay afterward for some shopping. I broke out in a sweat as soon as we stepped outside after eating. There was that telltale head-swimmy feeling. S. and I have been together a long time. One look at me and he knew what was going to happen. I started up the hill at a fast walk, knowing

I'd be winded and drenched by the time we reached our building. I made it, but it was another couple of hours before I could even think of leaving our flat.

The police went apeshit that afternoon and started gassing Causeway Bay while I was at home recuperating. By then, we were used to seeing tear gas and baton charges and water cannon and mass arrests at the end of the individual protest marches and demonstrations. The cops were already corralling people, boxing whoever was around into alleys and such, then arresting them all. Guilt by proximity. This was the first time the cops had been so indiscriminate in a busy shopping district full of bystanders in the middle of the day. Tourists. Kids. Grannies. Regular folks just out there to buy some T-shirts at Uniqlo or H&M, or kitchen shit at Ikea; or to eat dumplings at Din Tai Fung. The live footage on TV was appalling, people running this way and that to escape from the advancing cloud-walls of tear gas and the cops in their dystopian sci-fi black battle gear. Screams and shouts. The distinct thump of tear gas canisters being launched. Swearing in Cantonese. More screaming. Endless screaming.

If we'd gone over there on time and as planned, we'd have been caught up in that. Probably gassed, possibly captured and beaten. In the strangest of ways, my punctuality issues saved us that day.

Falmouth, England: June 2021

As expected, there's plenty of parking at the station near campus. I send a quick text to the group chat on Teams: *I'm almost there, I'm walking!*

Quick response from one of my colleagues: *There's only one guy.*

The rest aren't here yet.

Coping strategy: Like many gay men, I walk fast. It's safer. Not that I fear being jumped here, but I've had the habit since childhood. You're less of a target if it's hard to catch up. A paved path leads from the station parking lot up to campus. In Hong Kong, this would be a bleak affair of bricks and sun-bleached street furniture, any plants pruned back to gasping nubs. Here, it's a patch of lush woodland, and the highlight is a *Gunnera* plant. Also called giant rhubarb, the thing towers over me and has leaves the size of umbrellas. I believe they're endemic to Venus.

Coping strategy: Harm reduction. I force myself to slow down. Instead of charging forward, I'm walking briskly. I slow down a bit more. It takes effort. Although this university and my previous one have very little in common, one thing they share is an insidious slope. You don't notice until you're out of breath and uncomfortably damp. If I have to be a few minutes late, I can at least arrive dry and still able to breathe. Composure helps. So does oxygen.

There's a lot to unravel, a lot to unpack. I'm rarely late for things here now. I think of all the times I've exasperated people in the past. I think of my Colombian-Italian friend from Hong Kong who's in Riyadh now. Whenever we'd get together, I'd tell him to arrive an hour earlier than I meant for him to be there. Sometimes two. Nobody needs these strategies here, not with me. Nobody's going to get mad at me today, but the anxieties capering in my head aren't about that. In one form or another, I've been protecting myself all this time.

The group of teachers arrives in the room five minutes after I do. Even masked, I've got my breath back. More or less.

"What *is* creativity?" I ask once everyone has settled in.

We begin.

THE THINGS WE TAKE
WITH US ARE RARELY
THE THINGS THAT
WE'LL NEED

Let's talk about ceramic knives. I'm convinced I shouldn't move to England without one. I don't want to arrive in my new home and have nothing decent to slice with. Ceramic blades cut like lasers but I'm worried about chips and breakage. Durability. We're in the Wing On Department Store in Sheung Wan, downstairs in the household-goods section: neither Hong Kong's most upscale hypermarket nor its most gentrified district. If you're the sort of oddball who loves random finds like lavender tea from Sri Lanka or breakfast cereal from Poland, this is paradise. Let's talk about the crowds, though. On a normal not-too-hot summer Saturday, we'd be deep in a sea of shoulders and elbows. But the pandemic's not over; it's barely begun. The rest of the world doesn't know how ugly things are going to get. Here, everyone has a mask on. People keep their distance. The viral nightmare started just a bullet-train ride away, up in Wuhan, and Hongkongers have already endured a year of urban warfare. The terror and fury have taken their toll. Everything is chipped and broken. Everyone talks about leaving. It's hard to dwell on that for very long, so let's talk about household goods a little more. Let's talk about washing the soles of our shoes when we step inside our apartment: the cleaning station we've set up beside the door; the products we keep there. Although the spray we use to scrub our shoes might not remove the dioxins left over from the expired tear gas the cops have been blanketing the city with, it's better than doing nothing and tracking slow death and tumors across the living-room floor, which we now mop every other day. I put another package of disinfectant wipes in my basket. I am glad to be leaving, and relieved, and scared, and tired of this city I also love. Everyone understands. They feel the same way: depleted from the constant danger, dreading further conflict. And yet it grinds on. There are rumbles, clashes, days it's not safe to go out—still. There's no telling how long it will endure, how long we will have to endure it. So let's talk about Tiffany's, which is a few blocks away. Wing On and Tiffany's have very little in common except for one thing: when you're there, nothing bad can ever happen to you. Even if I'm feeling chipped and broken, my hunch that I need a new ceramic knife is likely to be correct. I pick one out. Black handle, white blade. It will feel good in my hand. If I had to, I could defend myself with it. And let's talk about how eager I am to stop thinking this way.

TO THE BARRICADES (OR: WRITERS, BLOCKED)

1.

When your existence itself is a crime, laws become little more than rough guidelines: things to be questioned, worked around, or ignored altogether.

2.

We're going to talk about writer's block. It's a topic writers tend to avoid discussing, half curse and half contagion. This superstition has its roots in another, possibly older one: that of the muse, which underpins much of what we believe about how writing works and why it sometimes doesn't. What it boils down to is that secretly or not, many of us have habits or rituals to summon a Greek goddess who may not exist.[1] If she manifests and is pleased, she will send us into a creative flow state during which words will pour out of us like cold, refreshing Assyrtiko on a hot afternoon in Santorini. Hours will pass, pages will fill, but our hands will not tire. It's exalting when you experience it, but it doesn't happen on command. To an extent, it's beyond your control. Fallow intervals can be terrifying, which is why we don't like to discuss them much.

When I was a kid, I slipped more easily into that elevated, feverish momentum, writing story after story longhand on lined notebook paper. Although I preferred legal pads, which felt more adult because they had more lines and no holes, any sort of paper would do. A story would come to me. I'd scribble it down as fast as I could get the words out. By the time I was done, another idea would usually have formed in my mind. If I didn't start on it right away, I'd wait until the next day, never longer.

I began writing longer-form work back then too. My first "novel," to use the term loosely, was a linked series of stories about hyperintelligent cats who had their own flying saucer. They parked it in a hangar under a shrubbery in front of the house where they pretended to be pets. By day, they'd fly to random countries because you could get the best rosewater in Bulgaria or the best gemstones in Tanzania. I didn't know much about geopolitics then but I did love an atlas. These stories formed a narrative arc that involved a conflict

1 It was widely believed up until the late 1800s that poems and other works of literature genuinely were divinely inspired and had their origins in external sources. (Reynolds, 2015). Reynolds, S. (2015, October 25). Five reasons you're experiencing writer's block. *Psychology Today*. Retrieved from https://www.psychologytoday.com/blog/prime-your-gray-cells/201510/five-reasons-youre-experiencing-writer-s-block

with an evil scientist who had death rays and, of course, hated cats. I wrote this magnum opus in one of those hardbound blank books I suspect are often regifted. At some point, I graduated or leveled up to writing about humans: mostly fanfic continuations/ripoffs of Edward Eager's *Half Magic* and his subsequent books. The recurring themes: being hated for who the characters were, and of magic-enhanced escapes to distant places where they'd no longer be in danger. Or not the *same* danger, at least.

Since I still had to live through my subject matter, I was saving myself through these escapes into writing. The frenzy was my constant refuge, my hopeful blankness. One after another, I'd bash the stories out onto the page, show them to my parents and a couple of friends, lodge them in a notebook with the rest of my work, and move on to the next. I started reading *Writer's Digest* in my teens, so I knew what writer's block was: *a problem other people had.*

3.

I'm gay. I was born in North Carolina in 1970. Came out in my late teens. North Carolina had sodomy laws on the books until 2003, when the Supreme Court ruled in *Lawrence v. Texas* that they were unconstitutional. Although I was living on the West Coast by then, in a state that abolished its own sodomy laws when I was still in elementary school, North Carolina remains the standard by which I measure everything, even now, in my fifties, from the other side of the Atlantic. Obviously sexual activity and sexual identity aren't the same thing, but it takes more than a dose of saltpeter and a bucket of icewater to pry them apart. So in a sense, certain aspects of my existence were illegal until my early thirties. And depending on what country I visit, that's still the case.

As integral as sexual orientation is to my identity, I came out as a writer (so to speak) much younger: at age seven or eight. I attended a small private school, total enrollment less than two hundred. There was one teacher per grade, and she would teach every subject. We stayed in the same classroom all day except for recess and PE. That year, the teacher often gave us creative writing assignments. Since this was a thing I already did, I was happy to carry on doing it and getting As on my stories. One day, she asked several students to read our stories to the class. After mine, the kids all applauded. Fireworks went off in my head: *This is what I was put here to do.*

4.

To understand writer's block, it helps to know what creativity is. In a paper published in 1962[2], Sarnoff A. Mednick offers a useful definition: creativity is a complex problem-solving task. It relies on novel connections between ideas and bits of information. Although we tend to think of creativity in more abstract terms—self-expression! new ideas! the muse!—it makes sense when you think of it taking place in the service of an objective. If you watch those home-renovation shows, you (sometimes) see creativity in the designers' clever

2 Mednick, S.A. (1962). The associative basis of the creative process. *Psychological Review*, 69(3), pp. 220 - 232.

ideas for rearranging space and adding extensions. You see it in storage cubbies and cabinets in space that was otherwise wasted. Elsewhere, you (sometimes) see creativity in accounting, when CPAs expense everything they think they can get away with. While you're driving, creativity (sometimes) comes into play. Do you stay on the main roads, do you obey your satnav's directions, or do you veer off the beaten path if you know a better route? And in a political crisis, creativity runs amok: graffiti, slogans, artwork, a banned anthem. The problem is the government, or the lack of one.

In the arts, creativity is both more and less obvious. A book, a short story, a poem, a painting, a sculpture: we see the finished product, or perhaps the work in progress, but the creativity manifests in every minuscule decision the artist makes. Once you begin to think of the process as a series of objectives that will culminate in a finished product, this definition makes more sense. You're solving a creative problem, and the process of reaching a solution is complex, self-reflexive, and interconnected. Think of the thousands or millions of individual problems—some tiny, some not—that have to be solved in the course of writing a novel: punctuation, vocabulary, sentence structure, verb tense, paragraphing. Whether to convey information via dialogue or exposition, or some combination of the two. Minute shifts in perspective, point of view, and narrative distance. Character names. Which descriptive details will convey enough information without bogging the reader down. Larger structural issues of chapter length and composition. Framing and flashback. The overall narrative arc. Similar lists could be drawn up for any branch of the arts.

In any system as complex as this, something will go wrong from time to time. If creativity is a natural human process akin to, say, digestion or respiration, that means you'll get the occasional creative stomachache or case of the sniffles. To carry these metaphors3 a bit further, creativity is similar in its requirement for input if it's going to work properly. You can't write a novel without having read a lot of them first. Ideally, you will also have read poetry for exposure to language that is both beautiful and economical. You will have read short fiction to learn about efficiency in storytelling, and nonfiction to fill your head up with interesting facts. Perhaps screenplays for their lessons in structure and staging.

So it's normal and natural for the process to break down now and then. Like any other bodily system, it works until it doesn't. Moreover, the problem may not be a breakdown per se; it may just be that your problem-solving process is incomplete. You may need more input: time, solitude, company, art, literature, experience.

There's no muse.

5.

I lived in Hong Kong from 2008 until 2020. If you remember 2019's huge protest marches, I was one of those people in black. Although I never threw molotov cocktails at the cops or set train stations on fire (I believe the police instigated much of the violence in order to justify cracking down on the protestors), I was there for all of it. Even if you avidly followed those events in the media, you have no

---

3   These are only useful up to a point. There are obvious parallels between input (nutrients, air) and absorption and so forth. However, the end product is waste, whereas the end product of a creative endeavor is not, one hopes, nothing more than halitosis or shit.

idea how dark things got at the end, how violent and horrible, and how sinister the situation continues to be.

6.

Depending on which survey you look at, either Germany or Sweden ranks as no. 1 for recycling. However, there's another largely undiscussed venue for recycling: the writing community online. If you're reading this on a browser, open another tab and do a quick search on some phrase like "top tips for writers" or "how to write a short story." You'll get some crazy number of hits, nine digits depending on which search engine you use. Check the first few; compare what they say. You should notice the pattern right away: I'd guesstimate that about 95% of the writing advice you find online is recycled, albeit paraphrased and repackaged: Daily word counts. Butt in seat. Show, don't tell. No adverbs in dialogue tags. No two characters whose names start with the same letter. The muse. Find your voice. Be authentic. Stay in your lane. No matter how many times all this gets repeated and retweeted, these rules will not apply to every writer in every situation. Little is original and new.

During Donald Trump's grotesque campaign for the White House and the blur that was 2016 - 2020, the word "gaslighting" entered the public vernacular. Broadly speaking, to gaslight someone means to say things and behave in ways intended to make them question their own beliefs, even their own sanity. One form of gaslighting involves repetition. Repeating a lie won't make it true but it will wear the victim down; it will make them more vulnerable.

Now do one more Internet search: "writer's block is not real."

If you're one of the contingent shilling writing advice online in hopes of gaining followers, finding clients for your editing services, and/or building a readership for the creative work you should be doing instead of writing listicles, you're kind of proving my point. Repeating a lie won't make it true but it will wear a frustrated writer down. It will make them more vulnerable. To what end, though?

7.

There are three kinds of writer's block. (It's a real thing, by the way. There are equivalent terms in French, German, Spanish, and Chinese. The origins are disputed, but the notion that it's all a collective delusion or pathologized laziness has been debunked.[4] One is the most common sort: you just can't write. The second is more nuanced: you can crank out the words in forms other than your preferred one. The third is more about erasure: you can write but you loathe your work so much that you feel compelled to keep it from being read. I've been through all three, sometimes concurrently. At the time of this writing, I'm doing all right, but after I graduated from college, my creative work crashed to a halt. For about four years, I couldn't finish a story. It wasn't that I lacked tools. Back in the early '90s, Brother Industries made a word processor, the WP-80, that was basically a single-function computer. It was a single integrated unit with a screen, a keyboard, a slot for a 3.5" diskette, and a printer. No Internet, of

4 Castillo, M. (2014). Writer's block. *American Journal of Neuroradiology*, 35, 1043 - 44.

course. That wasn't a thing yet. But I had a lot to scream about and nothing to say. Those were very grey years, and I began to suspect whatever creative spark I'd once had, had gone out. Clearly I wasn't going to become the Famous Author I'd dreamt of being all my life. My personal mythology drifted in those years: it became more about comfort, agency, and a certain craving to be taken seriously than, well, *writing*. At some level, I understood this and became convinced I should go to law school. It wasn't the life I wanted, it wasn't the *career* I wanted, but it seemed to tick the right boxes.

Immersed in research, I forgot about stories for a while. Everything back then was slow and paper-intensive. You had to buy and flip through thick guidebooks for any educational program you were considering. Having done well on standardized tests all my life, I figured the LSAT ought not to be a problem. And hell, I'd actually study for it, which I'd never needed to do before. I used my Brother to make lists of the universities I thought I could get into and the others that might be a stretch.

The weekend before I took the exam, my messy alcoholic boyfriend came messily out to his mother. Instead of studying, I spent most of that Saturday and Sunday talking on the phone with him through tears and meltdowns. We lived in different cities, about three hours apart. Any closer and he'd have spent the weekend crying on my pillows between dashes to the bathroom to throw up. He was the kind of guy who'd be drunk by the time I got home from work, but being no paragon of mental health myself and searingly lonely to boot, I kept him around because the alternatives were scarier. Being required to take care of someone who was such a mess was comforting in a strange way, even if he could be demanding. The Monday of the test, I felt so anxious and unready that I couldn't keep food down. I ate two stalks of celery that day. While I didn't bomb the LSAT completely, my score came back about 20% lower than I had expected—not enough to rule out law school altogether, but enough to keep me out of the better programs.

Serendipity saved my writing career, such as it is. I wasn't looking for calls for submissions but happened to find one in the classifieds of some gay magazine or newspaper—maybe the *Washington Blade* or *The Advocate*. The editors were compiling an anthology of LGBT-themed ghost stories. I grew up in the rural South surrounded by folklore and crazy people. There was no lack of material. I'd been away long enough to have processed it more. I figured if I couldn't come up with something for this book, I might as well call it quits. A couple of days later, a story idea sprang to life in my head. It took me a few days to write it. I printed it out and faxed it to the editors on the day of the deadline. A couple of months after that, the acceptance came in the mail. The breakthrough I'd been desperate for. My first sale.

I really came that close to giving up.

8 .

Block, blockage, blockade.
  Black bloc.

9.

Since then, I've maintained a consistent writing output. I've been called prolific, but I don't think that's a fair assessment. I'm not Joyce Carol Oates. I don't do this full-time. I'm not even sure I want to. I cherish the relationships I've formed with colleagues and students. I enjoy the camaraderie of writing conferences; I also enjoy the subtle art of lacerating dickheads who ask keynote speakers paragraph-length questions. I run a small press, too. It's not the cornerstone of my identity, but I'm comfortable with my layers and complexities. Apart from that interlude in my early twenties, I've never had an existential crisis because I know what I'm here to do and the rest is either a bonus or expendable.

There are fallow periods and false starts. Any number of half-finished short stories drift like tendrils of goldfish shit toward the bottom of my Google Drive folders. Two of what Anne Lamott would call "shitty first drafts" of novels languish there as well (okay, perhaps I'm not done with the digestion metaphor). Someday I might revisit the more recent of the two, as I like the underlying premise very much, but it won't be a black mark on my soul if I never get around to it. I'm all for writers supporting each other, but the idea of announcing my daily word count online fills me with a gassy sort of horror.

10.

The protests in 2014 came about because Hong Kongers were expecting a democratic "one man, one vote" [sic] election of the territory's Chief Executive. Beijing made it clear this was never going to happen, something more people should have seen coming. When you've lived in Hong Kong long enough and your social circle is more local than expat, you learn things. Case in point: when Margaret Thatcher was negotiating the Handover terms with Deng Xiaoping, apparently he told her that under no circumstances would a direct democratic process for the territory's leadership ever be acceptable to China. And if she were to press ahead with such reforms, he would use the full strength of the People's Liberation Army to take over the territory. If it took sacrificing millions of lives to get Hong Kong back, then he would pay that price without hesitation.

At the time, Britain could have obliterated China in about twenty minutes. It still could. However, the Falklands War had just happened, and Thatcher felt there was no public appetite for prosecuting another war over a colony so far from home. Better to cut losses and compromise. Hence, the actual language of Hong Kong's Basic Law (the document that serves as the territory's constitution) is more aspirational than binding. In other words, it smells like democracy and tastes like chicken.

I was out there the night the protests started in 2014. I had just started my job at the university where I would work for the next six years. Somewhat naively, I felt that if my students were out there getting their heads bashed in by the cops, I should at least be there to bear witness.

I don't think anyone imagined how bad things in 2019 would get.

11.

In his studies of writer's block, Robert Boice identified six negative emotions that may cause or exacerbate the condition[5]:

- Internal censorship
- Fear of failure
- Perfectionism
- Residual trauma from negative early experiences with writing
- Procrastination
- Mental-health issues

I have written a book-length, diary-style manuscript on the 2019 protests and their 2020 fallout. The working title is *Blood and Black T-shirts: Dispatches from Hong Kong's Descent into Hell 2019-20*. Not elegant, but it gets the point across. I documented everything, including the dark shit that never made it into the international news. But I've been warned not to publish it.

I'm mildly concerned that no one will take it seriously. I'm used to not being taken very seriously. I used to rant about that on my

5   Boice, R (1993). Writing blocks and tacit knowledge. *The Journal of Higher Education*, 64(1), pp. 19-54.

blog when I was trying to sell a book proposal about why the 2008 financial crash was going to happen and how if you were a member of Generation X, you should strongly consider leaving America before it did. The two or three replies I got from agents were dismissive at best: *You don't know what you're talking about. You don't have the credentials to make a claim like this.* The subtext: *Stick with writing gay thrillers.* I left the US in 2005. In 2008, when the global economy tanked, I was in Hong Kong. Every day on my way to work, I'd walk through Hong Kong Station and discreetly gloat at the red numbers on the stock tickers on the big video screens overhead. Mass financial collapse has never been so fun and affirming.

Am I a perfectionist? Yes and no. I have a master's in linguistics and have run a small press for ten years. Bad punctuation annoys me. Sloppiness annoys me. Pretty much everything annoys me, if I'm honest. But sometimes you have to make a conscious decision to be done with a piece of writing and move on to the next project.

Residual trauma from negative early experiences with writing? Yes, I can see how that would be a problem. All the years people spend trying to get published. The starvation for that crucial, validating first byline. The negative experiences came much later in my own career.

Yes, I procrastinate. I prefer having written to the desolate, swamp-draining slog of actually doing it. No one writes because they enjoy it; they do it because they must. If they're in the so-called zone, they're in a state of creative euphoria that lifts them out of the drudgery of the keyboard. There are times I just can't. I'd rather read, take a nap, or hang out with the cat.

As for the mental-health issues, I'm going to sidestep a bit and refer you to Alice Flaherty's magisterial book on the subject, *The*

Midnight Disease: The Drive to Write, Writer's Block, and the Creative Brain.[6] She does a better job with this topic than I possibly could.

1 2.

To be clear, the 2019 protests were not riots. For the most part, the marches remained disciplined and orderly because that's how Hong Kong rolls, or used to. The mounting violence at the end was down to the police and the mainland paramilitaries embedded with them. Dispersal operations at the end of the marches soon turned into vendettas, then open hostility toward the public. There was a wantonness to them, a mindless slashing evil the likes of which I had never seen before, much less thought I'd have to live through. As weeks turned into months and the government dug in its heels, the stories turned darker: insidiously at first, then out in the open.

These things happened, or some version of them did: gang rapes in custody—young men as well as women; beatings so bad that shattered arms hung from black-clad shoulders like sacks of glass shards; rendition across the border to black sites up in Shenzhen and Guangzhou, certainly for torture and possibly for organ-harvesting; burning prisoners' eyeballs with laser pointers while in custody. Kettling protestors and passersby, forcing them to kneel in stress positions for hours, then hauling them away by the dozen. Tearing off masks to pepper-spray protestors' eyes and faces. Attack-

6   Flaherty, A.W. (2004). *The midnight disease: The drive to write, writer's block, and the creative brain.* Boston & New York: Houghton Mifflin.

ing commuters in metro stations for the crime of being in the wrong place at the wrong time, probably killing a few, subsequently covering it up, and desecrating the memorials citizens put up and maintained. Kids were dragged out of food courts in shopping malls, out of elevator lobbies in their own buildings. The cops teargassed the whole city for weeks on end, perhaps thinking mass civic torment would turn the populace against the protests. It didn't work, so the motherfuckers kept on gassing.

Toward the end of this nightmare, a journalist friend told me another story: the string of "suicides" among younger protestors—dozens of them—was actually a series of murders. The common denominator? They'd all been arrested and mistreated in jail, and could serve as witnesses should there ever be Nuremberg-style trials. Detainees from wealthier families were pressured to leave Hong Kong. The ones who couldn't afford to do that were flung from tall buildings or drowned in the sea and left floating. The official explanation was, of course, to blame the protests. That's typical for Hong Kong under this regime. But young people began carrying notes to say they would not kill themselves in custody, and on getting arrested they would shout their names and *"I am not going to commit suicide!"* in case they turned up dead later. The cops quickly got in the habit of covering people's mouths upon apprehending them.

A Telegram group was set up in an attempt to locate people who'd gone missing. There were hundreds, it seemed. Possibly thousands. Although I couldn't read the Chinese details and descriptions, I could see faces. Most were young. In half an hour of scrolling, I recognized at least four of my own former students.

1 3.

As a Southern writer, I have always been fascinated by place, and I tend to write the kind of stories that wouldn't be likely to happen in other locales. The debate around cultural appropriation—who is entitled to write about what—has made me reflect on my own choice of settings. A few years ago, I put together a spreadsheet of my short stories and novels: where they were set, where I was living when I wrote them. A pattern emerged, a gap of approximately two years before my default location setting shifted to wherever I was living at the time. For much of the time I lived in Washington DC, I still wrote about North Carolina. When I moved to Northern California, I kept on writing about DC. Once I knew San Francisco more intimately, it became the primary setting for my work. In the same way, this work habit followed me to Portland, Seattle, Seoul, and Hong Kong.

At least in fiction, I'm still not writing about England; I haven't been here long enough; I'm not quite ready. But two years have passed since the horrors of 2019. The *place* was already there—I spent twelve years in Hong Kong and considered it home—but to say the *subject* has found its way into my work would be a bit of an understatement. There's been no lack of material. I've been away long enough to have processed it more. Now that I've escaped to a distant place where I'm no longer in danger (or not the *same* danger, at least), I should be able to write about it. Shouldn't I?

14.

Black bloc.
   Writer's block.
   Blockages.
   Barricades.

15.

The (creative) writing has been on the wall for some time now. In 2015, the creative writing MFA program at City University of Hong Kong was abruptly shut down. Although the stated reason was that it was losing money, it was a self-funded program. CityU's administration charged the program to use classrooms, theater space, and other facilities... and, according to a well-placed source, kept changing the rates, sometimes retroactively. Malice and incompetence are ugly cousins.

As is often the case in the Potemkin financial hub, the official explanation ignored the obvious: many of the MFA students had been participants in and supporters of the protest movement. The international, low-residency nature of the program attracted students from all over. And—troublesome foreigners!—they went on to write about what was happening there, and published widely.[7] This attracted the wrong kind of attention.

Early in the 2014 protests, the writing spray-painted on a wall at my own university read, in English and Chinese, *Are you going to keep silent until you die?*

16.

Negative emotions, updated for present-day realities in Hong Kong:

Internal censorship: If I publish anything, there will be safety issues. I've already been warned by one author who used to practice law that this is "NSL stuff"[8] and I should shut up. Another has told me to try essays first and see what happens.

+ Fear of failure: Will anyone actually publish this?
+ Perfectionism: What if I get something wrong?
+ Residual trauma from negative earlier experiences with

7 Canadian novelist Madeleine Thien, who taught on the CityU MFA program, wrote about this in an article that was published in *The Guardian*: https://www.theguardian. com/books/booksblog/2015/may/18/why-hong-kong-is-clamping-down-on-creative-writing

8 The NSL is the National Security Law drafted and enacted in Beijing in 2020 without consultation with or input from Hong Kong's elected officials. In the eyes of the international community, this act marked the end of the "one country, two systems" treaty with Britain under which Hong Kong was supposed to manage its own affairs without interference from China.

writing: Living through it in the first place was more than traumatic enough.

+ Procrastination: (I'll get to this bit later.)
+ Mental-health issues: I have PTSD again—I was first diagnosed with it back in 2004 and recognize the symptoms— but the strain of the Covid pandemic means I won't be able to obtain a formal diagnosis via the NHS until sometime later, eventually, maybe.

Taking all this into account, I probably ought to have writer's block, but I don't.

16.

Writer's block is at least partly a crisis of expectations.

There was a boatlift to Taiwan so that protestors could escape. I found out about it a couple of months before it made international news.[9] One of my more politically active friends told me that unscrupulous boat captains would take money to help these young people flee to safety. They'd get within sight of the lights of Kaohsiung, the southernmost major city in Taiwan and the closest point to Hong Kong. A mile or so from shore, these boat captains would force their

9   The *New York Times* broke this story in December 2019. I think it was incredibly irresponsible of them to publish it, and by doing so, they put people's lives in danger and likely led to the high-profile arrests that took place in 2020. https://www.nytimes. com/2019/12/08/world/asia/hong-kong-taiwan-protests.html

passengers to get out and swim the rest of the way. Never mind that that wasn't what the young refugees were expecting. Quite a few of them drowned.

As far as I know, no one has written about that. Not in English, anyway.

1 7 .

I keep almost having ideas for short stories. I have a few titles in mind, but the necessary fusions and combinations don't happen as often as they once did. It's rare for a fully formed story to present itself to me: usually the process is more like a cascade of connections, one idea merging with another, meiosis as well as mitosis. There's no end to the metaphors I could mix. They're all valid and they all fall short. The stories are in my head somewhere. In the meantime, there's the novel, the essays, and the academic projects. I am content. If writer's block is a crisis of expectations, it's still real. The only solution entails more time and more input. More connections have to form. Sometimes you drown.

1 8 .

When I started writing this essay, I planned to list Hong Kong writers, journalists, and academics who have lost their jobs because of the political situation, because of their writing. Because they are being blocked. However, some are personal friends: still there, still in the maws of the territory's so-called legal system. I decided to omit this part for two reasons: naming them would add to the jeopardy they're already in, and in the time it has taken to write this, several more names have been added to the list. I can't keep up.

19.

The first Hong Konger was convicted recently under the National Security Law.[10] No jury. Three judges handpicked by Carrie Lam, Hong Kong's Chief Executive, who has continued to insist that freedoms of speech and the press remain intact. As is often the case in Hong Kong, the official explanations elide the obvious: the NSL has outlawed anything and everything the government and its puppet-masters don't like. It is absurd and it is vile; it is stupid and it is a travesty. Malice and incompetence are ugly cousins.

Erasure is the third form of writer's block I identified in my research.

20.

"No intelligent man has any respect for an unjust law."
Robert A. Heinlein, *To Sail Beyond the Sunset*

---

10   https://www.amnesty.org/en/latest/news/2021/07/first-nsl-conviction-beginning-of-the-end-freedom-of-expression/

21.

I'm not okay. I function, but I'm not okay. I know I can't go home. My home has been torn away from me. England seems to be my home now. I feel sort of at home here. I'm no longer in danger, or at least not the *same* danger, anyway. I should be able to write about that, shouldn't I?

22.

When your existence itself is a crime, laws become little more than rough guidelines: things to be questioned, worked around, or ignored altogether.

Block, blockage, blockade.

Black bloc.

Barricades.

Repeating a lie won't make it true, but it will eventually wear an authoritarian government down.

I promise to obey the National Security Guidelines.

I promise to obey the National Security Guidelines.

I promise to obey the National Security Guidelines.

THE AFTERNOON ADMINISTRATION (OR: MY GRADUAL UNRAVELING, ONE CAPSULE AT A TIME)

27. Ginger

Until now, I hadn't known you could get ginger in pill form. A bottle's a few bucks at Whole Foods. When you're on a plane and turbulence hits, ginger ale helps. I imagine this does the same thing. It's worth a try. I've been nauseated more or less since childhood, a self-devouring ouroboros of IBS and anxiety. The one creates and consumes the other. I'll take a couple of these and see what happens. It can't hurt any more than my stomach already does. Besides, turbulence often hits. I've got to start looking out for myself. I'm not a kid anymore. So I tell myself.

29. Probiotics

Probiotics remind me of milk, and not in a good way. As kids, my sister and I called the acidophilus stuff diarrhea milk. A nice cold white glass of good germs, helpful but vaguely awful at the same time. Those days are long gone. Now I'm lactose intolerant. I could handle milk and cheese until one day I couldn't. But there's something new wrong with my gut—not my baseline instabilities, either. Continence is all I've got left to lose. Confidence? That was never there in the first place, and the last of my dignity went down the drain maybe a month ago. What's the worst that could happen? (I already know.)

29. Milk thistle

I'm careful with my diet and don't officially drink much, but ibuprofen is vitamin I. It's hard on the liver. Living is hard on the liver. My joints are shot. I work out regardless. Milk thistle repairs liver cells. I've read studies. It apparently works. And—let's be honest—I'm sure I shouldn't wash those NSAIDs down with a glass or three of red wine, but you know. Repetitive strain injuries, bad knee, something wrong with my neck. Disembodiment must feel amazing. Numbness *in excelsis*. That most sublime absence.

35. Fiber

I'm not dead yet, but I am in Korea, and you don't go out for a meal here without guzzling beer and/or soju: before, during, and after. The only time you don't is when there's wine. The cuisine's spicy and delicious but rather lacking in green vegetation. My system is calm now, excessively so. Big change from my constant distress and emergencies. I've switched to bran cereal and brown rice, and now these things. The grass is still brown on the other side too. If I'm halfway through my thirties and already taking fiber, does that make me middle-aged?

46. Turmeric

Plantar fasciitis, says a friend from my PhD program when I share my diagnosis on Facebook, hurts worse than childbirth. She's had it before, and she's had seven kids. Every step is a stout nail hammered into the ball of my left heel. I limp now and sometimes stop to sit down, shuddering and weeping from these sudden, intense spikes of pain. I am reduced to this. Turmeric is said to help with inflammation. With reductions and debilitations. It had better be, because plan B involves arsenic.

48. Glucosamine, chondroitin, MSM

This time I've pinched a nerve in my neck *and* blown out my left rotator cuff at the same time, a feat I wouldn't have thought anatomically possible. It hurts to turn my head. It hurts to *not* turn my head. It hurts to move. It hurts to *not* move. The physio helps and the painkillers dull the worst of it, sort of, but everything turns to clouds and mist with shard-cliches of lightning bolts and broken glass slashing through the fabric of what passes for reality. Anything that might repair joints tendons connective tissue *corrective* tissue broken bits and pieces holy Christ I swear I'll buy it by the truckload: apologies, I'm not myself. I don't recognize this person that I am. Pain is a physical construct. It is a cage, and the bars are electric.

51. Bilberry

The hammering pain is a thing of the past, but night-driving scares me and makes me feel old. It shouldn't, or maybe it should: British roads are narrow, and I'm American. Down here in Cornwall, there isn't much street lighting either. It gets *dark*. Then there's the mizzle: the local word for the drizzly mist that drifts from the low grey ceiling, obscuring everything. Wipers are useless against it. As if that weren't enough, I'm in my early fifties and have spent the last three decades looking at screens. By the end of the day, my eyes can't be assed. Everything else has worked so far, more or less. I can manage. Let's give this a try.

This is the afternoon administration. I take pills in the morning as well. There's a story there, written in capsules and tablets. What's next? Valerian so I can sleep at night, saw palmetto for when my prostate goes? Gingko biloba for that creeping absentmindedness? Rhodiola, ginseng, ashwagandha? I don't know how the story will end or who I'll be when I get there, only how the next chapter will feel when it sticks in my throat going down.

EMBODIMENT: A NUDE
RUMINATION

1.

There are dates and there are dates. I met Taeyang several months after moving to Korea from Seattle. He was darkly handsome, as if he eschewed the Asian ideal of fair skin and liked getting a tan; and a light mottling of acne scars lent his face a ruggedness it wouldn't otherwise have had. He worked for an NGO and was always on call. On the first date, we had dinner and a few beers at a forgettable restaurant in central-ish Seoul. At the end of the night, just before the dash to the subway station to catch the last train, he took my hands, looked me in the eyes, and said, "I want to be in a relationship with you."

"You want to see me again?" His formal manner and polite conversation had struck me almost like a job interview. Where in the States I was from. How I liked Korea so far. Had I learned any of the language. Could I eat with chopsticks. Could I eat with *Korean* chopsticks. The questions people usually asked, in other words. To the extent we had anything in common other than being gay men in our thirties, it was a lack of any talent for subtext.

There almost wasn't a second date. He kept cancelling plans. He'd message me to meet up at this place or that, then text with regrets at the last minute because his boss needed him to run an errand, regardless of what else he had planned for the evening or how late it was. I'd almost given up on seeing him again. Then he called one night to ask if I was free and drove down to my flat in the suburbs. Stayed overnight. Disappeared again. Several more months passed.

"I want to make it up to you," he said the next time I heard from him. "Do you have plans for Chuseok?"

Chuseok, a holiday that loosely parallels Thanksgiving in North America, tends to involve travelling back to your hometown to visit relatives. Taeyang's parents were dead, and his brother knew he was gay, so he saw no reason not to buy me plane tickets for a long week-end in Gwangju. There were ATM-like ticketing machines in shopping malls and major subway stations around the city. He stopped by one after work, fed it his bank card, and voila: e-tickets. He emailed me the details and said he'd pick me up at the airport there.

Gwangju is a major city in the south of the country. The population's about 1.5 million. It's known for being the site of a major pro-democracy uprising in the last days of South Korea's dictatorship. It's also known for good restaurants. We walked around the city center. Despite Gwangju's historic importance, there's little to see beyond the jumble of shopfronts and mixed-use buildings you see everywhere in Korea. I could read the language well enough by then to identify shops and restaurants: Barbecue. Pool halls. Bars. Banks. After-school tuition centers. The city's new metro line interested me more than anything else. He obliged me by following me into a station so I could say I'd seen it. Then he surprised me again:

he'd booked a night at a B&B out in the countryside. It was decorated in a traditional Korean style, he told me, and the owner would serve us tea—not the same level of ornate formality as a Japanese tea ceremony, more of a tasting session with a lifelong enthusiast who took Korean tea seriously and had a passion for sharing it.

Some family emergency erupted about an hour after we arrived. We had just enough time to walk around the village—mostly low red-brick houses that looked more Western than Asian—and survey the bleakness. Grey sky, distant hills, not much else. Taeyang had to hurry back to Gwangju, leaving me to chat with the host (whose English was about as fluent as my Korean), read, and eventually fall asleep. Although it was only October, it was already bitterly cold: still a degree or two above freezing, but with a gnawing, persistent damp. The Korean antiques in the house were lovely but the house was drafty and the bathroom was a miserable annex around back. Cold tile floors. No insulation that I could see. No proper shower either. Basically a toilet, a sink, and a hose. When I washed off before bed, my breath steamed in the air. There was apocalyptic shrinkage. I don't recall eating dinner.

After a breakfast of *doenjang jjigae* and grilled fish the next morning, Taeyang told me not to bother taking a shower. He'd decided to make it up to me.

"I'm sorry, that was awful," he said in the car.

"I didn't want to say anything about the bathroom, but..."

"No, it's okay. We're going to an oncheon to get warm."

I felt a mild twinge of alarm. You've probably heard of Japanese onsens, the hot-springs resorts one finds around the country. An oncheon is the Korean version: a bigger and more lavish version of the public bathhouses that are a part of daily life there. Although I'd been in the country seven months by then, I had never been to one of these. No one had offered to take me, for one thing. Now and then some of the other expats I worked with went to one, I think. But they were squeamish about inviting the gay guy. Afraid I would look at their dicks. (They weren't wrong. I just wouldn't have been obvious about it.) If I'm honest, though, the getting-naked part made me nervous. Gang showers in gym locker rooms: not my favorite part of working out. This would be much like that, only more so.

It's a holiday, I told myself. *Everyone will be at home with their families. It won't be too crazy.*

The town of Damyang is famous for its bamboo market, Taeyang went on to explain. We'd visit the oncheon there, get clean and warm, and then go into town for a light lunch. There'd be just enough time for him to drive me back to the airport in Gwangju for my flight back to Seoul. And if I missed it, it didn't matter: I could just take the next one.

"We're almost there," he said, slowing down.

Two guys in high-vis vests were directing traffic into vast parking lots. Think football game. Think rock concert. Think panic attack.

"So... umm... what's the etiquette for this? How does it work?" I asked, my throat thick from anxiety.

On the way in, Taeyang explained: we'd take off our shoes first, hand them over at the counter inside the men's sauna, and get locker keys from the attendants. The idea was to keep the floors clean. Then we'd get undressed, stash our stuff in our lockers, go into the bathing area, and take showers. You don't get into a hot tub without washing first. It's beyond vulgar. It's not done. Once we were naked and properly clean, we could dip into any of the tubs we wanted: hot ones, cold ones, mineralized ones, herbal ones. When it was time to leave, we'd wash off again, get dressed, and head out.

The place itself was familiar and not. If you've been to a gym, you know what a locker room looks like. This one was bigger, cleaner, more spacious: designed to accommodate hundreds of people, not a few dozen. There were benches between each row of lockers so you could arrange your clothes and put on your socks without bumping into a nude stranger with your backside. Heated floors kept the place warm. The men behind the counter were what Koreans call *ajosshis*: gruff uncle types who've seen it all but don't say much. I could make out about half the items on the menu pasted to the worn counter-top: bottled water, soft drinks, squid, eggs baked in the heat of the saunas.

An American friend who had recently left the country after a terrible job experience caused her to have a nervous breakdown had given me half her stash of Ativan in exchange for a cheap suitcase I no longer needed. I had them with me. When Taeyang went to use the toilet, I washed one down with a bottle of spring water.

If this had been Seoul, I'd have stood out less. I'd been in Korea long enough to navigate glances. Adult men and teenage boys would notice but not gawk. Little kids would stare and sometimes point. Older men would also watch me, but less intently. Enough of them had served with Americans in the war and afterward that naked white men were not of much interest. It wasn't just the nudity, though: I'm tattooed, which was taboo then, and my navel is pierced.

I prayed the pill would kick in.

Back from the restrooms, Taeyang seemed not to notice I was taking my time stripping off. Or, more likely, he did but was too polite to comment. *Here we go*, I told myself. Shirt off. Pants down. Undershirt. Socks. Boxer briefs.

Perhaps it was the Ativan or perhaps it was just a rare moment of sanity: naked, I couldn't feel the weight of the stares.

I followed Taeyang into the bathing area and had another mild panic attack: it was enormous, the size of an airport terminal in a small city. About the size of Gwangju's, come to think of it. And it was *packed*. Enough steam hung in the air that I couldn't see the far end of the place, so I couldn't guess at the number of naked men and boys. I could, however, make out that they were all the same color. Even by Caucasian standards, I'm vampire pale. I won't say a hush descended when I walked in because it wasn't loud to begin with. A few very young boys were chasing each other around in the foggy distance, shrieking and giggling until someone barked at them to pipe down. In all likelihood, the blip of silence was my own surge of terror, the kind that feels like pressure on your eardrums and your bowels, not a reaction from the other men present. It wasn't about me, and it absolutely was. After a second, it passed.

Unlike the pong of a gym, the air smelled mineralized somehow, or medicinal. It smelled like an Asian pharmacy, not a restroom. We turned left for the showers: dozens of the conventional standing-up kind—no partitions, of course—plus a row of the ones where old men sat on stools to wash off. Having soaped up and rinsed ourselves, we found a tub that wasn't too crowded and got in.

There were questions, of course: Was I American or Canadian. Was I an English teacher. How did I like Korea. Had I ever been to an oncheon before. Was the water too hot for me. Did I like spicy food. But these interrogations tapered off faster than they would have with clothes on. We were there to relax and get warm. If anything, the prevailing sentiment seemed to be approval. To the extent that people were noticing me, it felt more like *Good for him* than

Aren't their dicks supposed to be bigger?

After half an hour or so, I needed to take a leak and felt confident enough to go find the restroom by myself. That word (*hwajangsil*) was either the first or second I learned in Korean. As I made my way from the toilets back into the bathing area, I was wondering whether etiquette required a quick shower. Probably so, I reasoned. For cleanliness. And then I felt the hand on my back, between my shoulder blades.

"What the fuck?"

Whoever it was—some random guy—pressed hard and swiped down. I thought he was going to push me or grab my ass. I jumped. Then I understood: he was either trying to figure out whether my tattoo was real, or he objected to it, thought it was fake, and wanted to wipe it off. I didn't get the chance to ask. He kept going, disappeared into the steam.

Taeyang apologized when I told him about it afterward, and a couple of the men in the tub with us tsked and shook their heads in disapproval. Oddly enough, I felt validated. If the tattoo on my back provoked more reaction than the rest of me, it meant I had less to worry about than I thought. And if it was meaningful for these boys and men to stare at me, then so be it. We spent about an hour and a half there, all told, and then Taeyang decided it was time to get lunch. There was a restaurant in town he wanted to try: they served a local version of bibimbap inside a hollow shaft of bamboo. You couldn't pass through Damyang without having some. The rest of the day passed in a more normal fashion: the town, the meal (not bad, actually), the shops and markets we browsed in before the trip to the airport. Everything pivoted for me that day, but it would take years to recognize the actual extent of it.

2.

It's not hard to fuck up at being an expat. At the end of that first year in Korea, I had saved enough money to spend a month traveling around Southeast Asia. Or so I thought. I'd factored in the refund of my pension, an employer-matched scheme you could withdraw upon leaving the country. It wasn't much, just a few thousand dollars, but it was meant to supplement what I already had in the bank and get me through the summer until I could start my new job in late August. I should have known it would take twice as long as the pension agency's website said it would. Mea culpa.

The trip itself was more extravagant than any other I'd ever taken: a few days in Hong Kong, then on to Cambodia for a week and a half, then Malaysia, Singapore, and back to Seoul via Taipei. The high point—literally—involved climbing temples at Angkor Wat. I also glommed onto a Spanish-language tour group just in time to hear the guide's remarks about a cock-shaped obelisk in one of the temples. He referred to it as *el aparato*. The low point was spending more time in Kuala Lumpur than anyone really needs to, flying down to Singapore from there, and discovering how low on cash I really was. It wasn't an emergency quite yet but it was going to be a problem if the pension rebate didn't come through in the next couple of weeks.

The guy I was dating (not Taeyang, although he hadn't faded completely out of the picture yet) grudgingly let me crash with him when I got back to Seoul. My plan was to do that until I could find a job at one of the monthlong summer English camps in some other part of the country. For kids, these are wretched affairs: four weeks of intensive lessons during the summer and winter breaks. For Korea's expat English set, they're a way to top up your savings. They provide housing and at least one meal a day, plus (at the time) a few million won. That worked out to a few thousand dollars. If your camp is run by a competent director, you can have a good time. If not, well, you get the idea.

The day I got an offer from one in Jeonju, a midsized city about an hour north of Gwangju, my grandmother died. My mother emailed with the news. Although I wanted to rush back to North Carolina, I couldn't. There was the money. The distance. And my mother's determination to have her in the ground as soon as humanly possible. Finding my grief repellent, Seung-hyun stalked out of the apartment. I assumed he was sick of me. I was sick of me. Friends in Seoul, aghast at Seung-hyun's behavior, invited me out for dinner and beer. We had a spicy octopus dish. I knocked back a few pint bottles of Cass. Later that night, Seung-hyun came back drunk and apologetic. He just couldn't handle grief, he insisted. He just couldn't.

My funds came through the next day. While he was at work, I packed my suitcases and cabbed over to the Hamilton Hotel in Itaewon, Seoul's foreigner district. Before I could start my camp job, or the one at the university in two months' time, I had to hop over to Japan to renew my work visa, which you can only do outside of Korea. I'd take the bullet train down to Busan, stay overnight, and catch the ferry over to Fukuoka in the morning. The consulate there could process a new visa in one day. I'd pick it up the same afternoon, travel back to Busan the next morning, take the KTX back to Seoul in the evening, catch my breath for a day or two, then travel down to Jeonju to start at the camp.

I chose the Hamilton because of its sauna. Also because I liked Itaewon—it's Seoul's gay village, or one of them—but mostly it was the sauna. The night I spent there before heading down to Busan, I spent a couple of hours soaking. Unlike the airport-terminal expanse of Damyang, the Hamilton's sauna is more like the basement of a cathedral. Stone walls give the impression of a much older structure than the hotel two floors up. Fake stained-glass windows add to this effect. There are maybe five hot tubs; in Damyang, there was too much steam for me to see them all, much less count them. The water isn't so hot it will cook you, as well, and at least one of the tubs contains sulfur. You can stay in a bit longer. Although you will smell like an omelet after bathing, the minerals are great for fatigue and sore muscles. It's a better space for contemplation than a small studio flat with someone who doesn't want you there.

This was only my second sauna in Korea, but I felt less awkward now. I was naked. I was alone. There's an honesty in that. I didn't want to be stared at, but I was in decent shape and not hideous. Flashbacks to childhood: my father went on a brief fitness craze and dragged me along to the gym. I couldn't have been more than five, maybe six. Got a boner from walking around naked. Instant disgust from my father. He dragged me out of there almost immediately. Cancelled his membership too, as I recall. As I got older, my body was the subject of constant discussion and negotiation: I didn't walk the way boys were supposed to; I had no hand-eye coordination at all. I was so thin, too thin. Eat a sandwich. Put on some muscles. You walk like someone shoved a purse up your ass. Don't fart or the sperm will come out. And yet, I was on the municipal swim team and fast enough that serious conversations were had about trying out for the US Olympic team. My body existed in a constant tug of war between failing to meet certain expectations and exceeding others. Yet there was that layer of shame simmering under it all, that deep well of horror and awkwardness. In general, it was safer not to be noticed, much less looked at directly.

A busy few days later, I was back in Seoul with a new visa plastered to one page of my passport. I took the train to Jeonju; a woman from the camp met me at the station, took me to the apartment where I was to live for the next month, and after I dropped off my bags, took me to dinner and stopped by a tremendous supermarket on the way back afterward. I filled up two carts with the crap that I'd need: a coffee maker, and plenty of coffee; an iron and an ironing board; laundry detergent; enough food for a week. Extra toilet paper, I think, and a couple of towels. And staff from the camp kindly helped a Canadian colleague and me find a gym near our building. It had all the machines that we needed. Better yet, the locker rooms contained saunas with an assortment of tubs. Seeing that, I signed up on the spot.

That month exists in my memory like a bubble in time, or a glass dome. The edges are hard. They're protective. I did very little in that interval except work (great kids, great coworkers, great director, great city), read, exercise, and soak in the hot tubs. I seemed to have very little to say. I'd go after the camp ended for the day and spend a couple of hours. Weekends would be busier: older men would come in and do stretching exercises in the sauna, never bothering to venture into the gym. One day I saw a man doing lower-back stretches on the stone ledge of one of the hot tubs. He was straining to get his legs over his shoulders. His anus looked like a starfish doing jumping jacks. I looked away.

I was in the best shape of my life after that ascetic month in

Jeonju. Gym five times a week. Minimalist diet: lots of sushi, lots of vegetable stir-fries. Red wine, of course, strictly for the antioxidants. Grief and disruption burned off any spare weight I'd been carrying and gave way to a tentative peace, if you will. An embodiment.

3.

I met Robert for the first time standing in a crossroads just outside of the Byeongjeom subway station down the street from my building. I'd just started at the university. Didn't know my way around. But we were right at that spot where the suburbs gave way to the countryside. There were rice paddies on the other side of the station. It was late summer. You didn't dare stand still for more than a moment or else a typhoon of mosquitoes would engulf you and bite your face. Robert: white guy of Levantine provenance, muscular, on the pretty side of handsome. Also American, as it turned out.

"Can I help you? I live down the street and don't know where anything is, but you seem lost."

He had just started at another university in the area and was meeting colleagues at a bar up the street. I recognized the name of the building.

"You should join us," he said, and I did.

Over the course of the evening, he dropped enough hints that he was gay too—he name-checked bars in Atlanta and New Orleans— that I didn't see the next bit coming. By this point we were back at my flat drinking wine. He admitted he'd probably be happier calling himself bisexual, but he'd had a bad experience with an older man, and his parents would never approve. Therefore, he was hoping to find a girlfriend and settle down.

He'd already joined a gym in the area, and suggested I check it out. Just up the street from my apartment, it was small but clean and new, and well-enough equipped that I didn't hate it. It lacked the sauna facilities I'd enjoyed in Jeonju, but it would do. The first day Robert and I agreed to meet there, have a workout, and get dinner afterward, he finished before I did and went to take a shower. A few minutes later, he sent me a text: *I forgot my towel, would you get one at the front desk?*

Not a problem. I picked one up. Brought it back to the shower area. Was mildly taken aback by the size of what he clearly wanted me to see. Had to work to keep a straight face and not stare. To this day, I'm still not sure I succeeded.

Now and then we'd get together for a workout, dinner, drinks. Sober, he'd sometimes remark "I know you think I'm bisexual" out of clear blue nowhere. But a pattern was emerging. If we were showering after the gym, he'd angle himself so that I couldn't not see. It's one thing to shoot the shit with your friend in the locker room, showering or getting dressed after. Guys do that. It's another thing to position yourself to seek out your best angle and lighting, then taking your damn sweet time to wash your semi-hard *aparato* in front of a semi-captivated audience. I understood enough Korean by this point to know I wasn't the only one noticing.

We caught a movie one time. Went to the men's room first. He stood far enough back from the urinal that anyone passing by the open door could see what he had, draped over his fly.

I never commented. Although I liked the guy, I could tell he wanted he wanted the attention. I was beginning to think he wanted it from *me*—most likely so that he could turn me down and tell himself that made him straight. He'd talk about his exploits with women until we were a few drinks in. His guard would slip. He'd talk about the bars again. Eventually it came out that he'd even had a boyfriend before, in a dim high past he wished he could disown and relive in equal measure.

When a position in my department opened up, I encouraged him to apply. He got the job and found a flat much closer to campus, and within walking distance of my own place. He also found a gym much closer to home. Easily ten times the size of the one we'd been using, it had full sauna facilities on two floors, plus an acreage of shiny new equipment. It was Jeonju all over again: an entire hammam's worth of hot tubs, steam room, hot sauna, the works. I signed up on the spot. Winter was coming.

Although it was a much longer walk to the new place, and the trudge through a subfreezing Korean night could physically hurt by the time I got to the gym, there was a certain confluence. The sharp night air woke me up. That peculiar borderland between the paddyfield countryside and the new highrise suburban zone had a certain allure: the pitch-black park I had to pass by, the blocks set aside for development and squared off for construction that never seemed to get underway, the glow of the streetlights and signs ahead, the big blocky Korean letters. There was a Samsung appliance shop and a small Kia dealership. Various restaurants that always seemed to be closed. Late at night, a constellation of frozen *ajosshi* spit on the black pavement would sparkle like a mirror of the cosmos overhead. Repugnant, but still oddly beautiful.

Some of these nights, I'd meet up with Robert at the gym. We'd work out, shower off, have a soak. Unlike those timid expat guys from my first year in the country, he wanted me to see him naked, wanted me to stare. Almost *needed* me to, if I'm honest. Two years earlier, I wouldn't have had the composure. I'd spent too many years unable to inhabit my own skin, blanking out and going *tharn* from attacks on the street, beatings and insults at home. You run like you've got a dick up your ass. You're so skinny, I can't see you if you turn sideways. Your father and I know you're not like that. Don't worry, we're going to take you to a whorehouse when you get older. Make a man out of you. Scalded by much of my own existence, I empathized with Robert. I didn't want to have sex with him, but I sort of hoped that our unperturbed soaks in the mineralized tubs would maybe… alter his brain chemistry? Sitting naked with him night after night in the sauna, I mostly stopped caring that he had porn-star proportions and I was more like the cameraman. It rankled me now and then but I wasn't *suffering*.

We'd go out for beer and fried chicken on a lot of these nights. Pitchers of Cass, a whole hatchery's worth of chicken. He'd drink twice as much as me and stumble home in the cold. By this time, I'd found a job outside of Korea and was making plans to leave the country. As things seemed to be coming together for me, Robert was increasingly a mess. He'd made a new circle of friends and was burning through his savings buying them drinks at hooker bars in Itaewon. He blacked out and lost his wallet once or twice.

The last time I saw him, he stopped by my office to ask for a favor. He'd been with a prostitute on one of these nights out. Somehow the condom came off. He thought he'd caught something. Wasn't sure if he needed to get checked out. Would I take a look? Before I even got the words "I guess?" out, he'd unzipped and hauled out the problem. I felt like an apprentice mahout. The trunk clearly needed medical attention. I didn't touch it. What do you say to someone who is closeted, self-aware, and *choosing* to suffer? As for me, it wasn't that I needed to come out; I needed to come back in, in a sense.

Most other people's lives are not out-of-body experiences the way mine was for so long. Friends visiting from Dubai or Singapore or Malaysia would generally be down for a sauna visit and not shy about hanging out naked, something I'd never have proposed doing before that first oncheon visit. My architect friend from Singapore and I sat on lounge chairs at the Silloam Sauna near Seoul Station watching an impossibly handsome Japanese man soap down before his own excursion into the tubs. He knew he had admirers. We knew that he knew. There was a grammar to the glances, to the body language. No one said a word. On another occasion, the same friend and I left the bathing area of a different sauna in Gangnam just in time to see a man carefully blow-drying his penis with a hair dryer. He lifted it, stretched it, moved it around. Pure performance. Also terrifying. We used towels, and howled over beers later.

If this were a different sort of essay, the kind that reads more like a geometry proof or perhaps the closing arguments in a courtroom drama, this is where I'd put the quod erat demonstrandum. I'd talk about my newfound and enduring comfort with my body, about how nonchalant I've become in the locker room. But no one wants to read intellectually dishonest blatherings about a middle-aged white guy who moved to Asia, took his clothes off, and Learned Wisdom. Setting aside the obvious Orientalism, that's not how things even worked out. There were the lockdowns. All the gyms closed. I moved to England. I drive more and walk less. I'm north of 50. Entropy's roots burrow deeper. I was in excellent shape before the pandemic; now, not so much. For a while, the old unease retreated, or it went into remission. It never really left, though; it just pivoted back.

ON THE PLEASURE OF
FUCKING LOATHING
(AFTER THOMAS
HAZLITT)

There is a pair of raptors (always a pair, you see, or more, because in this war zone of a city, a lone raptor would be torn limb from limb by the furious public) in the concourse at Central Station. Incongruously, they're standing in front of the cookie shop. Sweetness and horror. The raptors are Hong Kong's riot police, black-clad horrors from *The Matrix* or some other, more recent dystopia. They're ostensibly cops. Only they're not. We all know they're shock troops from the People's Armed Police, or PAP: a paramilitary security force that's supposed to operate only on the mainland side of the border. I feel a bit sorry for them. Considering where they're from, there's no chance they understand what their presence here means. According to other rumors, which I also believe, they're high on some form of speed at any given time. If I were to meet these guys in some other context, I would probably like them. But that won't be possible here. Due to the brute violence, Hong Kong's protestors will not give up the demonstrations. Whoever is orchestrating all this will not give up the principle or essence of hostility. I think this way because I can't see the raptors' faces. The reflective tape over their visors makes them non-human, alien, *other*. I regard them with a mixture of horror and sheer fucking loathing. In a hundred years' time, perhaps the writers and thinkers of the day will excoriate us all as an ill-omened tribe unable to see beyond arbitrary borders, to set aside a politics of annihilation in the face of a much greater emergency.

If antipathies are the nature of nature, the conflagrations on the city streets most nights are about something more than unruly locals tossing petrol bombs at black-clad riot cops, pissing on the front gates of police stations, and occupying the airport. This is a push-back against mass stagnation, against a despotic surveillance state, against suppression. Or am I reading too much into it? It could just be a secret affinity for evil—what Orwell would have called "a boot stamping on a human face – forever." The difference between resistance and evil is a matter of perspective. I am not wearing boots.

Increasingly here in Hong Kong, crowds cannot assemble without being attacked. It used to be a joke here (and might still be) that if locals saw a queue, they would join it without knowing what it was for. A queue on the street meant a giveaway, something free. They didn't mind standing twenty minutes in the city's subtropical swelter if it they'd get an ice-cream at the end, or a bottle of cough syrup, or shampoo. And there have always been assemblies. Back in the distant high past of, oh, six months ago, there would be a march every other weekend protesting some new or old injustice. Traffic blocked in and out of key districts while people marched, carried signs, and shouted slogans. But now the whole town runs from the fire, not toward it. Executions *have* gone forward in the next street, the next MTR station, the next housing estate. There will be a price to pay for all this. Hatred is immortal.

That strange cur, that idiot, that crazy woman would be set upon if she were here in Central Station. My fellow commuters regard her just as I do: a public nuisance, of no benefit whatsoever. She will not step down. How has she not stepped down, even as the public in our millions have marched and vented our spleen upon her and demanded her resignation? If she were here, it would take more than two raptors to protect her.

The mind abhors a vacuum. Two months after I moved to Central, the police gassed my neighborhood. It was the spirit of the age, or perhaps just the spirits: I might have had a glass or three of wine that night, and vindictive humours got the better of me. I marched out of my building, down Caine Road, and down the escalator to the site where a phalanx of police had assembled, riot shields up. Half the people in the crowd had their faces hidden behind Guy Fawx masks. No one was going to be burnt in effigy that night even if it *was* Halloween, but in our terror and our hate, there was quite a bit of shouting. Havoc, dismay, wrongs, revenge: setting root here between two sects, two parties in politics, was a deadly animosity. I could feel the full force of that hatred toward these faceless, otherworldly devils in urban combat gear who would have had no compunction about beating me or my new neighbors into broken, bloody submission. The last trammels of civilization had worn thin; the veil of humanity, on being pulled back, proved to be flimsy. I suspect there are no faces under those visors.

So Mrs Lam, that celebrated idiot, that strange cur, makes long calculations in her own interest. Her husband and sons are known to have British passports. No one in Hong Kong's upper pantheon actually has to stay in the territory to live with the consequences of their work. More importantly, nor do their children. So Mr Ho, that scheming agitator, celebrated the gangsters who exploded hell-fire in the aisles of an MTR train in Yuen Long on July 21, to the astonishment and horror of the entire city. What strange beings these two and the others like them are, not content with doing all they can to hurt and vex their fellows here! If I were a praying man, I would call upon the Almighty and entreat Him/Her/It/Them to cast these traitors into the everlasting gulf of penal fire. Their malice begs eternity but that isn't long enough to suit their infinite spite, the relentless doom that their actions warrant. In the meantime, they and their masters continue attempting to control the opinions of others and to frighten the public into conformity by untrue words and monstrous denunciations; and surely worse is yet to come.

The pleasure of fucking loathing these people is in itself a form of nutrition. I despise religion because in America it has descended into a brainless cult of spleen and bigotry; it makes patriotism an excuse for carrying assault weapons into schools, restaurants, and shopping malls; there is nothing of virtue in it, only a degrading performance carried out primarily for the sake of censoriously watching over others and castigating them for their actions and motives. This is not a religion, this hatred I feel; it is not a cult or a creed. Nor is it evil, if we look closely. We revenge injuries against the frailty of the civic body. We hate old friends who support the political establishment; we stop speaking to them. We hate old books if they're little and red; we hate old opinions if they're of the same provenance; at last we come to hate ourselves for being mired in this nightmare for so long that we see strangers when we look in the mirror.

It has been painful to observe the exodus: many whom I have known casually if not intimately, on some friendly footing, have broken up and dispersed. If they have not already left Hong Kong, they are making their plans, discussing contingencies. Before long, they will be scattered like last year's snow, to Singapore, Canada, the US,

Australia, the UK, Malaysia, Taiwan. At least one will be dead, although I am mercifully unaware of this now. By the standards the rest of the world is used to, middle-class professionals here are rich. Some have got places in districts like Wan Chai and Taikoo Shing and Tsim Sha Tsui, bought when property was cheap and now worth millions. Some came as expats years ago and have grown quietly wealthy in business or the civil service. Times are changed; we and our quondam associates share in the city's continual alarm. It is distasteful; the stomach turns against it. What was good about the city becomes stale, and our repeated cancellations of plans because of battles and blazes in the streets leads to misunderstandings and ill-blood.

Even though Hong Kong is home, we take a certain dislike to this place that we love. The city is defined by departures. In a single day not too long ago but well before All This, six different friends and colleagues told me they were leaving: two bound for London, two for New York, two for Singapore. Yet another has bought a flat in Bangkok, as you do when you're gay and thinking ahead to retirement. Well before All This, the honeymoon period with Hong Kong comes to its end: we tire of the dripping, miserable heat; the ostentatious wealth in the streets; the ridiculous lives we all lead. One friend just bought a fourth flat because the estate agent spotted him walking by, knew he would like it, and ran outside to catch up with him. His business-minded mother lent him the money for the down payment. Another friend has grown tired of buying property in Hong Kong and is now focusing on Portland, where real estate costs a third what it does here, and is twice as big. Still another is vacationing in Gstaad this month. Skiing. Gigabytes of photos are forthcoming. Last month, he was in Kyoto. The month before that,

Beijing. The month before that, Toronto. If not for Facebook, one would lose track. In fact, one still loses track. We take a fond dislike to this place, this playground, these people, because life here gives us more than anyone should rationally have even as it also pulverizes us with its demands and contradictions and impossibilities. We will fight for it but no one wants to retire here. Pleasure requires more effort than pain and a better financial planner. It is easier to talk about why Hong Kong infuriates us all than it is to say why we love it, why we take to the streets week after week. Deep down, no one cares about Hong Kong, a local friend once averred. Everyone has foreign passports and a certain amount of money. We can leave. But these events have proved her wrong.

I am heartily sick of my own old opinions. I have good reason: ever since I got teargassed, I can't stop coughing. Once I start, I can't seem to stop. My lungs have been shredded. To liberate Hong Kong, this revolution of our times requires more than a bawd in a mask. Liberty is not a name but an intention: this system of tyrants and slaves will not stand; it cannot. And yet, I hold fast to my doubts: if certain political leaders wished for what is right, they could have had it long ago. They do not want to be kings of free people. The world is not worthy.

Instead of being patriots and friends of freedom, these two raptors are here to rivet on the chains of despotism and superstition. Through the vista of future years, I expect to see friends and former students carried away on an infuriate tide, proscribed, hunted down: fresh cries from a new Inquisition. For now, we will not yield to this brute force, nor to the innate perversity and dastardly spirit behind it. England, that mouther about liberty, holds the tools of deliverance. But will it use them? Not to do so would be the height of hypocrisy, servility, selfishness, folly, and ignorance. Seeing all this as I do, this unravelling of the web of human life into meanness, wantonness, want of feeling, want of understanding, and indifference toward others, I hope I am not mistaken in my public and private hopes. Have I not reason to hate and despise these two inhumans as I pass them by? In this moment, I could not possibly despair for the world any more than I already do.

TASTING NOTES

I can't prove the jug wine my parents drank was bottled on its journey down a horse's leg but I have my suspicions. Now and then, I'd
sneak a glass, thinking the approach of adulthood meant I'd have to
acquire a taste for it. I did try. I even used it in improvised cocktails,
the oddest of which also featured vodka, rock candy, and lime soda.

A catastrophic night in high school with a bottle of Ernest & Ju-
lio Gallo Chablis should have put me off drinking forever but didn't.
It was better than my parents' Taylor Lake Country White, which
is to say my gag reflex didn't kick in until *after* I was aslosh with
the stuff. I spent that night lying on the floor, head spinning, later
throwing up in my dorm room's clogged sink (I attended a residen-
tial high school). The next morning, woozy in the depths of my first
hangover, I had to scoop yellow, reeking vomit out of the sink. I then
had to unclog the drain by myself, not wanting to ask our hall's resi-
dent advisor for help for fear of getting in trouble. It took a couple of
hours. I needed a shower afterward. It was as vile as it sounds.

In college, my friend Jim tried introducing me to red wine. A
senior, he was thinking ahead to adult matters. Wine coolers and
Budweiser seemed sophomoric. He'd found a bottle of something
tense and Italian at the supermarket. Bought it because of the label.
He'd even acquired a pair of proper wine glasses. I want to say it
tasted like raspberries and chocolate-coated sin with elegant notes of

blackcurrants, mercy, and angel sperm¾but that would be incorrect. It didn't taste like much at all: wet rust, perhaps, followed by a mid-palate slide into nothingness.

"It's like drinking butter," he said.

With effort, I swallowed. Shuddered. Was done with wine for a couple more years.

Jim, my sister, and I all ended up in DC after college. We didn't plan it; it just worked out that way. My sister had worked part-time for about a year in a local department store's wine and cheese shop. It didn't make her a sommelier, but she could pick out a bottle. She insisted that real wine tasted nothing like the plonk our parents drank. Occasionally, she'd make recommendations. Ironstone Obsession, for example, went down like a glass of gardenias, sugary but a step up from the Bartles & Jaymes wine coolers we guzzled as undergraduates.

An afternoon trip to the Maryland Wine Festival resulted in sunburns and quaffable discoveries. Chambourcin, a grape variety mainly grown on the East Coast, convinced me red might not be so bad after all. But I rankled at feeling I needed to check with my sister for wine advice: What goes with chicken? Cabernet Sauvignon has too many syllables, so should I be afraid of it? Is the expensive stuff actually better? This should have been something I, as a proper functional citizen of Grownuplandia, could handle myself.

Although I couldn't afford it, I subscribed to the *Washington Post*. Like owning at least one black shirt and buying French roast coffee because it was "French" and therefore upscale, reading the news every day felt like measurable progress toward the authentic façade of adult sophistication I was desperate to construct. Having grown up being told our mother's parenting philosophy involved keeping my sister and me as naive and sheltered as possible for as long as possible, I had reason to be desperate. My impostor syndrome had impostor syndrome. People on the spectrum speak of feeling like aliens. All well and good, but feeling like an alien requires actually landing on Earth. You need a point of comparison. By my early twenties, I had barely set foot (or pseudopod, or tentacle, or tendril) off the mothership apart from a couple of aborted flights in low orbit.

One Friday, the *Post* published a review of Santa Barbara Winery's newest Pinot Noir. Although I'd browsed the wine reviews before, I always found the language pretentious. Flowery mouthbursts of moonlit Bing cherries picked at the peak of ripeness and then gently misted with Chanel No. 5, faint whispers of smoky tannins like the fog blowing through the Golden Gate, insidious hints of strawberries and upholstery and espresso served only in a cafe around the corner from the Spanish Steps in Rome. For the first time, it occurred to me to ask *What if these reviews are actually right?* So when I happened to find a bottle in an Annapolis wine shop the next day, I bought it. It must have been about twenty-five dollars then, well outside of my price range, but it felt important. My adulthood hung in the balance. If the wine was as delicious as the review suggested, didn't the twenty-five bucks count as tuition?

It took me months to work up the nerve to try it. It was enough at first to see it among the bottles in my makeshift wine rack, to know it was there, like having books by Thomas Pynchon on your shelves. The point was having them, not having read them. But those saucy tasting notes of Arctic cloudberries and gamma radiation and dusty libraries on quiet summer afternoons in the Upper South whispered to me. I'd been saving it for an occasion that never came: a romantic dinner with an interesting guy, a short-story sale, a lottery win. One night I just got home from work and said fuck it. Opened the bottle before I could talk myself out of it. Poured a glass. Took a sip. Took another. Although the Pinot didn't taste like believing ten impossible things before breakfast, it was, by far, the best glass of wine I'd ever had.

My Very Tense Friend (we'll call him the VTF) and I started out, as gay men do, casually dating. After a few months, the physical part fizzled out, but we liked each other well enough; we understood each other. A Midwestern transplant from a Czech family of modest means, he had moved to DC after grad school for a comfortable federal sinecure. Bored, well paid, and very secure, he sensibly bought an apartment and less sensibly bought a secondhand Porsche 944. He'd furnished his flat to resemble a tasteful gentlemen's club: functional antiques, broad leather sofa, minimal bric-a-brac. He liked the kind of red wine that had dusty labels in French, cost a lot, and tasted like sandpaper, ambition, and the tiny screams of grapes that died in a great deal of pain. Partly this was to do with his anxiety about being gay: he abhorred the chintz and frills and lace one found in some gay men's homes. But the other part was about his own ongoing upgrade. Like me, he was bleaching his blue-collar upbringing, albeit with more money and a few years' head start.

Being single, gay, and a bit slutty in a major city can be educational depending on what you set out to learn. From the VTF, I gained the fondness for quirky hotel restaurants, the weekend dash up to Boston with the top down on the Porsche (and the ensuing sunburn)...and the sense that someone who looked like him might find me worthwhile.

Later, the Swiss guy who worked at the World Bank changed the way I cooked without meaning to. I switched from fish sticks to monkfish, from canned corn to sauteed greens. There were afternoons at the Smithsonian. Ella Fitzgerald and Nina Simone on the CD player in the evenings. Then, at a party, I met the art conservator he dumped me for. We compared notes, made the connection, and started seeing each other at first to spite our mutual ex but after that because we genuinely got along. From *him*, I got an education in the basics: not just art, but wine too. Among other things, he introduced me to Bonny Doon Winery, which back in the '90s had a bigger range and lower price point. Vintner Randall Grahm's iconoclastic take on wine shaped my own: he eschewed supermarket standards like Chardonnay and Cab for Riesling, Viognier, and Rhône reds. Playful labels; serious wine. Later, there was the Venezuelan nurse who took me to Caracas. That's how I acquired my first passport stamp and my halting Spanish. Still later, the Taiwanese guy under whose amused scorn and tutelage I learned to use chopsticks. He also forged a check and cleaned out my bank account. I learned a lot from him. I learned a lot from all of them.

As a kid and well into my teens, I was never far from a humiliating memory: proclaiming I could talk to cats and making everyone cringe when I began meowing at one (it walked away), dodging spitballs thrown from the bus when it passed me as I rode my bike to school, jumping aside to get out of the way of incoming softballs I was intended to catch. There was the time my mother swung by the mall as she drove me home from the dentist. I'd just had several teeth removed in preparation for braces. We stopped in the craft shop I liked. She pushed me to apply for a job there while my mouth was still packed with gauze and oozing blood. The sales clerk looked as appalled as I felt. They didn't hire me. A lifetime of this awkwardness infused every step, every movement, every syllable.

Dinner gatherings with the VTF sometimes didn't end well. Although I didn't talk with my mouth full, bleed from an orifice, or fart at the table, I was always the odd broke guy who worked in social services and somehow didn't fit. At one such party, I misheard one of the VTF's other friends talking about where he'd studied: "Oh, I know someone else who went to school in East Stroudsburg. I didn't know you were from Pennsylvania."

He looked at me the way a frog looks at a beetle a split second before the tongue whipsaws out.

"*Strasbourg*," he said. "I was in *France*. Studying *French*."

How had I missed that? I blamed myself for yet again killing the mood with a reference to the mundane, and assumed everyone present blamed me too. The awkwardness was thick enough to spread on a bagel. It must have been me. It was always me.

A few months after that, at a gathering in Woodley Park, there was wine, banter, tastefulness. The couple who owned the house had spent time in Oaxaca. Everything matched, and didn't. My own apartment, a rental in a building decades past its Art Deco heyday, featured family hand-me-downs and IKEA's cheapest sadware. At some point, I needed to use the bathroom and asked where it was. Right off the dining room where we were gathered, it turned out. I ducked in, took a leak, and emerged to silence, pursed lips, and an inchoate tension in the air. It seemed I'd violated some unspoken social rule by actually pissing in the bathroom I was invited to use. The VTF confirmed this afterward, driving me home in his Porsche. Annoyed with me or embarrassed or both, he didn't sleep over this time. It didn't end our friendship, but there were no further invitations to dinner parties. I developed a mild fear of dinner parties, in fact. They often didn't end well.

Eventually, I played my adulthood cards well enough to travel. I'd only left America twice before this, to Venezuela and Vancouver. Despite these trips, it hadn't occurred to me that I could just buy tickets online, hop on a plane a few weeks later, and spend a few days in London. But when British Airways announced a fare sale, I did exactly that. No one chased after me with a net. I found this miraculous. It felt like escaping myself.

To make sure that pressurized 777 air didn't desiccate me into a fine powder, I shoved two 1.5L bottles of Evian into my backpack. You could still get them through security back then; 9/11 was still a couple of years away. I bought a buckwheat-filled neck pillow. The flight crew raised their eyebrows but, being British, didn't comment.

I can confirm I survived the flight and loved London. On my last night of the trip, I took a colleague's advice and bought dark chocolate bars as souvenirs, carefully avoiding sugary American brands. That's how I learned that if you don't have many good friends living nearby, there's no point bringing gifts back.

Thus began a program of travelling badly. Off to Sydney and Melbourne on the tail end of a case of giardia. I don't know what messed me up worse, the protozoans or the Flagyl I had to take to kill them. Despite a bodily presence in both cities, mainly I saw the public restrooms. I observed that people in Sydney tend to shit at public toilets, or toward them, rather than in them. But the zoo was nice. Next, I went to Singapore... wearing a day-old pair of Dr. Martens. I brought no other shoes along. They chewed blisters into my feet my first evening there. The next morning, I bought a pair of Merrills. Spent the next two weeks limping like the Little Mermaid.

I naively thought it would be okay to visit Madrid in midwinter and saw very little of the city due to a pall of pouring rain and jet lag. When I did venture out, I went to the big three art museums: the Prado, the Thyssen-Bornemisza, and the Reina Sofía. I wanted to love the Prado. Gallery after gallery of great works by Goya and Velázquez. In reality, I *liked* it, but I almost got mugged on the metro. My trembling before Titian had more to do with terror than Stendhal syndrome. On those cold, rainy afternoons I would stop back by my hotel, tell myself I wasn't going to fall asleep, fall asleep anyway, wake up at 2 A.M., and stumble out for a very late meal at a nearby Argentinean restaurant that stopped serving at four. "*Otra vez?*" asked the waiter my third night there when I showed up and ordered the chicken. Nothing went horribly wrong in Barcelona or Bilbao. I visited the Sagrada Familia, the Museu Picasso, the Fundació Joan Miró, and the Guggenheim. By the time I got back to the U.S., I was so exhausted that I cancelled the trip to Düsseldorf I'd booked two months later.

I also cancelled my immune system on that trip: I developed a fungal skin condition and shingles back-to-back. It took months to recover.

"*Slow down,*" my doctor ordered. "Are you trying to kill yourself?"

If travel and wine help you develop a convincing veneer of authentic sophistication, moving abroad glues the mask to your face. What, after all, could be more sophisticated than living overseas? So, when I was offered a teaching position at the Hong Kong campus of Shenzhen Arts University (not its real name, but ShArts is an apt abbreviation), I thought I had finally arrived and looked forward to the novelty of being able to put money into savings. A private university set up by an extravagantly wealthy family one colleague described as Hong Kong royalty, ShArts gentrified a couple of historic buildings in Kowloon, splashed money around on arts events, and opened their new campus for business. The family spawned legends, not stories: dinner parties back in the day with Madame Chiang Kai-shek, a network of private schools and a couple of colleges in the major mainland cities, galleries in Shenzhen and Shanghai, a private jet.

Because we had to submit our PowerPoint slides for review by the Vice President in charge of the Hong Kong campus (at least until he hired an assistant and made her do it), it was emphasized that we had to *make it pretty for ShArts*. Hence, images of Dufy and Chagall and Kandinsky and Miró served as backgrounds for my slides on writing skills and grammar. I used a photo by Cindy Sherman to teach countable and uncountable nouns. I used Takashi Murakami whenever I could, just because. Francis Bacon, Ai Weiwei, Andy Warhol: I loved it and then one day after seeing three of my new colleagues crying because of the workload and the spying and the nastiness simmering below the surface there, suddenly realized I hated it. Every day looked perfect and felt awful.

People whispered for fear of being overheard. An assistant would check classrooms to make sure we were in them ten minutes ahead of scheduled start times, take attendance (ours, not the students') at functions, take notes on what we were wearing, and covertly search our desks and computers. ShArts issued laptops configured to store everything on the university's servers instead of their own hard drives. Toward the end of my time there (I'd have said tenure, but ShArts was very public about not offering it), Madame President swanned in for a staff pep talk. Budget cuts loomed. Her driver was outside keeping the Mercedes running—for the air conditioning, of course.

"We've just got to... buckle down! Tighten our belts!" she said at the end of her remarks, smiling at us all and pumping a fist to emphasize the seriousness of the situation.

"Is your Chanel scarf this year's collection?" I asked.

No reason was given for offering to renew my contract only on a probational basis. To correct my unspecified shortcomings as a professor, I was required to have a six-week series of coaching sessions on the subject of professionalism. I began making my own chess moves, frantically applying for jobs and was even told I'd be getting an offer, but that position fell through at the last minute. Then the HR orc in the main office decided to fire me at the beginning of summer anyway.

Hong Kong was the most expensive city in the world before the government turned it into a dystopian hellhole and everyone who didn't get thrown in jail or murdered by the police started leaving. Hiring season at the universities had already ended. At least I had something in savings. I didn't think it was going to be enough.

Hong Kong's Labour Department runs a 24-hour hotline for people needing advice on whether job situations might be breaking employment laws there. *You need to take ShArts to court,* they told me repeatedly. *They can't just dispose of people like that.*

I filed the paperwork. I ate sandwiches. They were cheap. I lived on the thirty-third floor of my building. I sometimes wondered, looking out the window at the pavement below, if people falling from that height really died of heart failure long before hitting the ground. I'd read somewhere that they did. I was going to run out of money in a few months' time if I didn't find a job. Even if I won the court case and got a settlement, I was already buying groceries with my credit cards.

My friend Kelvin owned a prominent design firm and had done well for himself: a house near the beach on the south side of Hong Kong Island, a Porsche, plenty of money. Over drinks, he'd once cheerfully agreed with me that I'd never be able to buy property in Hong Kong on what I made there. The subtext: I should ditch my boyfriend for him. Improve my standards. Upgrade myself.

To cheer me up after learning I'd lost my job, he proposed brunch at a Provençal place in Soho followed by an afternoon at the beach. At the restaurant, when other guys began arriving, I almost got up and left. He hadn't mentioned inviting anyone else. I'd met a few of them before: chiseled bankers and marble-like architects and fortyish tech bros who'd coded their way into management: flawless mannequins who flung themselves from Gstaad to Berlin to Hokkaido to Cape Town in business class because they could. Bangkok for Songkran. The Maldives or Mauritius for a cheeky weeklong beach getaway. Buenos Aires because why not. Pleasure was, after all, grim and serious business. Rich and oddly joyless, these were the last people I wanted or needed to see.

Champagne was served. Salads arrived. Conversation turned to the topic of "managing staff out." One of these shellacked androids had been given a quota at work: every year, he had to fire ten percent of his team—not because they were performing badly, but because it kept them terrified, on their toes, striving, achieving. I kept my mouth shut. It was better that I didn't speak. I wasn't sure I *could* speak.

Après lunch, *la plage*. Drinks. Toward sunset, everyone ambled back to Kelvin's house, used the garden hose to rinse off the sand, changed out of swimsuits. One or two of the other guests had no qualms about stripping naked when they hosed themselves down, perhaps the better to show off their gym results; I ducked into the nearest bathroom for my own ablutions. Later, at the table, I learned they were going to spend a week in the South of France the following summer. They'd rented a house in Antibes. Did I want to come?

"I'll pay," Kelvin said.

Everyone looked at me. I mumbled something. Talk turned back to firing staff for fun and profit. It occurred to me that yes, in free fall, your heart probably does give out. How many of them knew I'd just lost my job? Kelvin must have told someone. But it's hard to think clearly with the wind roaring in your ears on your way down.

"I want your feedback on something," Kelvin asked the group as his maid brought out a fresh bottle of Sauvignon Blanc from a New Zealand winery I liked but couldn't afford at the moment. "Would you date someone who makes a lot less money than you do? Or consider having a serious relationship with him?"

"No!" came at once from the guy to my left, Trevor, a deeply sun-tanned Chinese Canadian finance executive. "Absolutely not. Why would you even suggest a thing like that? What's gotten into you?"

"There's somebody I like. I've been thinking about it, how it could work."

"Why would you want to support anyone? Why would you want someone who couldn't keep up and pay his own way? He's not... *unemployed*, is he?"

A couple of the living statues seated opposite were watching me now, not Trevor. We were seven at the table. I was utterly alone.

The Sauvignon Blanc had all the characteristics I needed in the moment: fruit-driven, punchy, and brightly acidic with steely notes of citrus and rage.

Fork or knife? The question abruptly ceased to be whether I was going to stab Trevor through the back of his right hand, which was next to me on the table, but which cutlery I should use. The knife would be cleaner. The fork would make more of an impression.

He carried on talking: "I don't even know where this is coming from. Keep him around for the sex, whoever he is. Throw him away when you get bored. Find someone who doesn't need a sugar daddy."

The fork, then. It was in my right hand.

The moment stretched out, elongated with possibilities.

This was free fall; this was the final second before impact. It was as vile as it sounds.

But no. I didn't have permanent residency yet, nor the money for whatever penalties I'd face. I'd be jailed, deported, ruined. There was the cat to think about. I set the fork down.

If this was sophistication, perhaps all I needed to be was *enough*. I asked Kelvin to call me a taxi, then finished my wine and poured myself a refill instead of waiting for the maid to do it. It tasted like vodka and rock candy and lime soda, and it was sublime.

BLACK NOON, BLUE
EVENING

Cold makes me anxious. Eastern North Carolina, where I grew up, doesn't get cold much. There was a blizzard once. Three feet of snow fell. No school for a week. It was white heaven. Thing was, our house hadn't been built to hold that much extra weight. The foundation buckled. My parents had to take out a second mortgage to have the timber support beams replaced with steel ones. But I was too young to understand those risks and expenses then. The fear came home and unpacked its bags a couple of years later when a prowler came scratching on a neighbor's window one icy night. The girl, home alone, called us screaming for help. My mother grabbed her gun and charged out into the dark, telling me to lock the door behind her and not let anyone else in, no matter what. The next morning, the cops found the dead, bedraggled body of a woman frozen into a nearby pond. No mention was made of a gunshot wound. My mother denied shooting her but there was a certain twinkle in her eye.

My first college apartment was the back half of a 1930s bungalow in Greenville, on Biltmore Street. The street name invoked historic mansions and the rusty electric strip heaters on the moldings invoked the fire station when they melted brown holes in the poly-cotton blankets that fell off our beds onto them. That was when I began to notice the numb patches in my fingertips. The way my hands slowed down and stopped working. Little feeling. No grip. I dropped things a lot and still do. It gets worse in cold weather. When the pilot light in our furnace went out one winter afternoon, the temperature in the apartment wafted grimly downward. Down, down, down, and my hands locked up, and I had to call someone from work to stop by and help me light it again. I couldn't strike a match or flick the ignition wheel on a lighter. My flatmate and I could see ourselves exhale. Even with the furnace working again, that house never really got warm.

Northern California, the first of the places where I spent my thirties, is notoriously chilly. For much of the year, the maritime fog that refrigerates San Francisco also snakes across the bay and cools the patch of Oakland where I lived. The heated towel rack in my bathroom kept my apartment warm on the brisk days. Now and then in those high-summer winters, I'd turn the radiator on. This entailed twisting the knob back and forth to see if anything would happen. After a few minutes, the thing would hiss if I did it right. Clanks and groans would ensue, followed by welcome heat. But I didn't do that often. The towel rack did most of the work. The problem, to the extent there was one, concerned placement, not noise or money: I began to worry it was too close to the commode. Was I drying myself with piss-misted towels? Some thoughts need to die in the back of the mind. I couldn't move the thing, so I sat down to pee and closed the lid when I flushed. The apartment stayed as warm as I needed it to.

Now, when I look out toward the horizon, the chilly midday pall puts me in mind of Seattle: hazy shapes left behind on a blackboard that's just been erased. My Seattle years were drizzly and grey, best left half-forgotten. At this time of year, the sun doesn't really come out. Like my cat, it's in hibernation; it naps behind clouds. Seattle, like southwestern England, is mild in the summer. Balmy. The chief difference between these two places, up till now, has been the direction in which the rain falls. In the Pacific Northwest, it drifts down. In the pointy little corner of the UK where I live now, it slashes sideways or pelters down in frozen form, little white pellets the size and shape of rabbit shit. It was darkish at noon today and the sun set around four. Seattle's on the other side of the world, but I'm not sure I ever really left. It's a matter of gradation. I was warmer there too.

It's frigid in this house. The wave of Arctic air blanketing Britain has everyone blue and shivering under duvets. There's snow here in Cornwall. It doesn't snow here often. My nose won't stop running and the cat hasn't budged from his heated bed since breakfast. A Persian, he ought to be insulated against these extremes. His behavior suggests the opposite, though. Faint ripples in his fur indicate that he's shaking. I turn the heat up. The grinding hiss of the radiator, not the alarm clock, woke me this morning and yesterday: sudden tension, the sound of pound notes on fire. Even though we keep the thermometer set on 15c and the space heater on low, I'm worried about the next power bill and the ones after that.

Although cold has always left me feeling hollow and uneasy, teetering on the edge of mortality, I've never liked heat that much either. My parents designed the house I grew up in, the one with the foundation that almost killed us, to be powered by renewables. Back in the '70s, this made them eccentric, not progressive. The wood stove could heat the whole place except in the coldest months. We also had heat pumps and fiberglass insulation. There was talk of solar panels but they were exorbitant then. Every so often, during eastern North Carolina's rare icy intervals, we'd bring the kerosene heater up from the basement. The house smelled like a runway in the morning and so did our clothes but we didn't asphyxiate in the night; and the utility bills, my mother boasted, were next to nothing. Those pink swathes of insulation scared me, not the bills I never saw. Don't touch that stuff, warned my parents again and again. The fibers will break off and embed in your skin. You'll have to go to the doctor. Stay away from it. *That* was scary.

In my twenties and early thirties, I developed repetitive strain injuries in my hands, shoulders, and neck. I was a sign language interpreter. That's one reason I left the profession. Most of the time, most of me ached. I saw any number of physical therapists, massage therapists, even a chiropractor. They gave the same advice as my trainer at the gym: alternate heat and cold. Ten minutes of one, then ten minutes of the other. Sure-fire remedy for strains and inflammation. I've been alternating between extremes for quite some time and should therefore have been purged of all stresses and tensions. I should be insulated from headlines about energy price caps and warm banks, about what leftovers from the North American bomb cyclone will do to the weather here. I've lived in five US states, the District of Columbia, and five countries now. Part of the calculus you make before a big move is whether you'll be better off in the next location, but the wind is screaming and I'm coming unhinged. Another gust, and the house creaks. In most respects, I've come up in the world, or closed a great circle. But everybody's talking about their bills and nobody's talking enough about the cost. There are bodies frozen into ponds here too and the temperature keeps dropping.

THEN, THE WHITE NOISE

1.

Faced with the impossible, all writers have is metaphor and tenacity.
Revisiting these places on the page,
Bloodstains on a white station floor.
Certain stories are impossible to write. They're too big. Words falter. The story demands to be told because there's no other way you can live through this if you don't get the words down on the page, or the screen. You sit down to write. The first sentence comes. Then an ellipsis. Then, the white noise.

2.

Intentions are both invisible and illegible.
We appall ourselves and then, seeking truth or perhaps expiation, we record our misdeeds, examine them, hold them up for others to see. Yet we now live in a world devoid of accountability and

179

consequence. Journalists were once our gyroscopes: as long as we had them, reality could right itself. Now they are our martyrs in high-vis vests, dodging pepper balls and baton charges, choking on tear gas, and sacrificing eyeballs to tell the world the truth in post-factual times. It's hard to tell the truth, yet we must continue to try.

3.

We're surviving. Except, a lot of us aren't, and won't. Consider: *enormous* and *enormity* are different words, except when they're not.

4.

Certain emotions are too big to write. They're impossible. Words falter. The circumstances demand a bloodletting of sorts, or a trepanning: you're a writer and you are consumed. The horror of wartime conditions: the collapses of logic and reason, the betrayals of the one and of the many, the shit-dirt ugliness of broken bones and bleeding faces. Empty eye sockets and skin rippling red from chemical burns and asphalt kisses. The vast sadness of abandonment: being shattered, and trembling in advance of the breakages still to come. Words are only stars in this cosmos of suffering. You can only infer the shape and size of this expanse by examining these individual points of dark. It's too big.

5.

Certain writers insist nonfiction isn't meant to be therapy.

After our first session, my last therapist asked me to write an account of the events that had led to my decision to seek counseling. After all, I was a writer, he reasoned. We could put that skill to good use. I agreed, and as instructed, I wrote everything down. Emailed it to him. And in our next session, he chuckled. Told me I was clearly very creative. There was no way all of that could have happened. It was too much. Normally people don't live through that kind of thing. They either kill themselves or fall ill and die.

"Let's talk about the parts I had to leave out," I said.

The body can only contain what it can contain.

6.

Although the writer may have some distance from the material—time may have passed, the world may have moved on—the act of telling the story reignites the embers. The world is the story and the story is bigger than the world. Although it might be urgently necessary to write about what one has been through, this is dangerous terrain. You should never use second person. Always think about the ending. Every story has one, even if you might once have thought otherwise.

7.

We write because we must draw lines under and through. I wrote a memoir about the first twenty years of my life. It took almost thirty more years before I could write it. The writing itself took one year. Let's talk about the parts I had to leave out:

...*white noise.*

8.

The setting of this essay is Cornwall:
+ Cliffs.
+ Seagulls and magpies.
+ Sunsets and seagulls.
+ Foxes.

9.

Certain stories and certain emotions are impossible to write. They're too big. We write toward them, and around them. We show outlines, maybe contours; we describe the sky by the shapes of the clouds as they drift across it, not the blue. The horizon confines us. Faced with this impossibility, we need assonance, consonance, repetition. Rhythm and enjambment. Punctuation. They're the glues that put our fragments back together, that let us reflect upon how this new assemblage might work and what it will mean. Try not to think about the ending. Every story has one. You'll get to yours, even if you might once have thought otherwise.

SUNSET HOUSE:
ACKNOWLEDGMENTS
AND SO FORTH

Well, I've gone and done something I'd have found surprising a decade ago: I've written an essay collection. When I was younger, nonfiction always seemed beyond me somehow. There's no logical explanation for that beyond seeing myself primarily as a fiction writer and never having worked much in other forms. After I finished my PhD—which spawned my most recent novel *Inhospitable*—I decided it was time to try my hand at nonfiction. To that end, I started the book that went on to be my memoir *I Wouldn't Normally Do This Kind of Thing*. After all, it makes *so much sense* to start out by writing a whole book in a new form instead of, you know, individual essays. I seem to have pulled it off, however.

The subject matter of this book is tough. As you will have noticed, much of it concerns the horrors I experienced in Hong Kong during the protests (please do not refer to them as riots) and ensuing state violence of 2019-20, and the global Covid pandemic that began in late 2019. I seem to have a knack for living through complicated material. If you've made it this far, you may be interested in knowing that I did end up getting diagnosed with PTSD and seeking therapy to put myself back together. I've also been diagnosed more recently as autistic, which puts an extra fun spin on all this. Am I okay? Have

I survived it all? No one comes through experiences like these unchanged, unbroken. I'd like to think I've come through a rough patch into a place of relative respite. I don't feel quite as unhinged these days. That's something, isn't it?

I'd like to thank a few people for helping make this book happen: Xu Xi, for being one of the first and strongest proponents of my adventures in nonfiction. My track record for getting these essays published would seem to have proven her right. Sven Davisson at Rebel Satori Press as well, for the continued support of my work. Calvin Malham, for the new chapter, and for remaining gracious and accepting through some very shambolic intervals. Joe Wilson and Greg Henry, for new community. The editors at the lit mags who accepted these essays, or wanted to. Finally, and with all the cloak-and-dagger you've come to expect, the people in Hong Kong I can't safely name but appreciate very much. Perhaps one day in my lifetime, that city will go back to being something other than an Orwellian grey area of surveillance, authoritarianism, disappearances, and mass emigration. My time there is over, as all but a few of my old friends have left. But I'll keep my permanent ID card in my wallet as a reminder and a small token of hope.

Persist, continue, carry on, resist.

Truro, Cornwall
21 July 2024